Journeys into Czech-Moravian Texas

NUMBER SIX:
The Charles and Elizabeth Prothro Texas Photography Series

Journeys into Czech-Moravian Texas

SEAN N. GALLUP

Texas A&M University Press
College Station

Frontispiece: Ammannsville, Fayette County: Local Innoc Tofel plays the Texas
Czech songs from his youth in the settlement's little saloon.

The paper used in this book meets the minimum requirements
of the American National Standard for Permanence
of Paper for Printed Library Materials, Z39.48-1984.
Binding materials have been chosen for durability.

Library of Congress Cataloging-in-Publication Data

Gallup, Sean, 1968–
    Journeys into Czech-Moravian Texas / Sean Gallup.
        p.   cm. — (Charles and Elizabeth Prothro Texas photography
series ; no. 6)
    Includes bibliographical references and index.
    ISBN 0-89096-751-2
    1. Czech Americans—Texas—Pictorial works.   2. Texas—Social life and
customs—Pictorial works.   I. Title.   II. Series.
F395.B67G35   1998
976.4'0049186—dc21   97-39310
                                                               CIP

Dedicated to the memory of my parents,

Dorothea Gallup, 1941–77,

and Stephen Gallup, 1939–96.

Contents

Part 4:

Preface

This book is the result of fieldwork I pursued for my master's thesis while I was a student in journalism at the University of Texas at Austin. My interest in the subject grew out of several factors: one was the six months I had spent teaching English in Czechoslovakia prior to coming to Texas, another was a strong awareness of my own ethnic identity as a German-American. And though I had heard about Texas Czechs from the first few days I was in Texas (driving past West on I-35), it was not until I met Toni Barcak of Velehrad that I became hooked.

I met Toni and her son one day while I was visiting her neighbor, Ben Jurica. The three were speaking Czech to one another, and during a lull in their conversation I asked her a question in English. She looked at me strangely, then nudged her son and said something to him in a low voice. Finally, in *very* broken English, she responded. Yet she had lived in Texas her whole life (born at nearby Novohrad)! The idea that, in 1993, a native Texan could make do with only the faintest grasp of English and rely primarily not on Spanish, but on *Czech,* astounded and fascinated me. I was then convinced I had to do some kind of documentary project on modern Czech Texas.

I began by driving out on weekends with *The Roads of Texas* in hand, looking for places like Praha and Velehrad just to see what was there. I also talked to scholars like Clinton Machann and James Mendl, and began doing initial research at the University of Texas libraries to familiarize myself with Texas-Czech history. In the summer of 1993, I met the Knapek family of Granger, and after that first full day I spent with them photographing and helping them to pull weeds from a cotton patch, I knew that the project had to establish a very personal connection to the subjects. I wanted to show who Texas Czechs were and what they were like, and at the same time show the culture in its different forms.

I knew that if I was going to do this, I would have to live in a Texas-Czech community. Initially I chose La Grange, though the recent boom in oil exploration had filled all the available housing. I wanted to be in either Fayette or Lavaca County because they provided the springboard that sent Czech settlers to other parts of the state and because Texas-Czech culture in the two counties is still strong today. So I chose Fayetteville, the "cradle of Czech settlement" in Texas, where I chanced upon Sherman and Kendall Macdaniels, Houston natives who had renovated a beautiful Victorian house and were willing to rent me a room for six months. In Fayetteville I attended the local chamber of commerce meetings, Czech singing group rehearsals, and the occasional community events. I also got to know Buddy Polansky, director of Fayetteville's museum, who introduced me to the Korenek family at Ellinger.

Throughout the project I knew I didn't want to focus too much on any one settlement or family because I wanted to give an accurate representation of how large and scattered the Texas-Czech population is. At the same time, I wanted to approach issues in depth, so I balanced the two considerations by searching out people and places that addressed topics I thought significant. I chose the Knapeks because they still farm cotton and speak Czech, even among the younger generation, and practice many Texas-Czech customs. The Koreneks still speak Czech and practice the customs as well, so I assigned representational roles to the two families: the Knapeks who still farm cotton and the Koreneks who adhere to old ways. In this way I determined what to photograph and when to visit.

From Fayetteville I covered the settlements from Caldwell to Corpus Christi for the mapping and concentrated the rest of my work in Fayette and Lavaca counties. In the spring of 1994, I moved to West for a brief period in order to map the North Texas settlements and cover another area of prominent Texas-Czech culture.

By the beginning of 1994, I also began making arrangements to go to the Czech Republic in order to follow Texas Czechs as they searched for their families. Especially because so many still speak Czech, I was curious to see how Texas Czechs and native Czechs would interact, and what kind of impression Texas Czechs would have of the land of their ancestors. Again, I needed a central base to work from, and I chose Rožnov pod Radhoštěm, located in northeastern Moravia and right in the middle of where many immigrants to Texas had come from. I also chose Rožnov because I had met the director of the folklife museum there, Václav Mikušek, who offered me a place to stay on the grounds of the museum. Rožnov proved ideal—not only did the Czech Heritage Society conduct its three-week cultural seminar at the museum, but nearly all of the touring groups of Texas Czechs came through there. I had made previous arrangements with some Texas Czechs to go with them when they searched for their families, while I approached others during my visit to the Czech Republic.

Some who have seen the pictures are surprised that I was able to gain access to a people many consider shy or suspicious of outsiders. Some older, rural Texas Czechs don't have much contact with strangers, so often I made an introductory phone call through the recommendation of a mutual acquaintance, which helped to dispel initial suspicion. I was also careful not to overwhelm potential subjects with too many requests. Most often I simply told them I was a graduate student from the University of Texas doing research about Czech people in their area, and was interested in doing a brief interview with them. If during or after the interview I thought there was also photographic potential, I asked them if I could take their picture or even come back to spend a day following them around with my camera.

Because I was driving to so many Texas-Czech communities, I decided several months into the project I might as well do a map to show Czech settlement in the state. This also provided an excuse to drive right up to people's houses and knock on their doors without prior notification. I would explain I was doing research and ask them to indicate on a very detailed map where they knew Czechs had and had never lived, though often the conversation drifted to stories about the community or personal histories. This is also how I got some of the portraits, such as those of Angelina Bednar and Fred Vinklarek.

Once people realized I was sincerely interested in them and Czech Texas, they were only too happy to talk about themselves and their culture. Often I also quizzed people on their use of dialect by asking them how they said certain English words in Czech, and many seemed tickled that an outsider should be interested in their language. Often at the end of an interview, a subject would tell me how happy he or she was that someone was doing research on their culture. Only once, from a woman in New Taiton, did I get an unyielding refusal to be helpful in any way, though I had the impression she had had an unfavorable experience with a prior researcher or journalist.

Often I felt I was working on a jigsaw puzzle without the box cover to guide me; I didn't always know which pieces were useful, I didn't know how many I would need for the completed picture, and I didn't even know if the image that was taking shape was the right one. I realize now I pursued certain topics in greater depth than was necessary, but I guess that's just part of documentary. At times I also felt I was venturing into areas of research that I had insufficient background to cover properly. I am, after all, not a linguist, cartographer, ethnographer, anthropologist, or musicologist, and I don't even speak Czech well enough to understand everything people said. So I decided to stick to my role as an inquiring journalist in making and analyzing my observations, both in the course of the research and in the write-up of this project.

I think a project such as this is important because it reveals a rich and still-flourishing culture that most Texans know nothing about. Yet, this ethnic heritage will change dramatically in the next few decades as the number of Czech-language speakers continues to dwindle. In this era that honors the multicultural nature of this nation, it seems the multicultural richness of rural America is being overlooked, much to the detriment of our understanding of what *is* America.

As I look over the manuscript now, I see it crying out for additional research by specialized scholars. The language, particularly, deserves more attention. At present, there are still enough Czech speakers in the state for a researcher to gain a firm impression of the diversity in dialect and even to put together a linguistic atlas of Texas Czech that mirrors the nature of original settlement. However, perhaps only a decade remains before the presence of Czech speakers in some areas will be only a memory.

Note on terms, Czech language spelling, and diacritical marks

Throughout this project I have tried to be as accurate as possible in the written reproduction of Czech language passages, though this has often created a difficult dilemma: I could write all the texts with appropriate diacritical marks according to proper Czech spelling, but to do so would not always be "accurate," per se, for two reasons. One is that the Czech language that has survived in Texas is heavily influenced by northeastern Moravian dialects that don't conform to standard Czech pronunciation. For instance, though the Czech word for sausage is spelled *klobása,* the vast majority of Texas

Czechs will pronounce it *klobasa,* with the short *a.* The second reason is that, because the English language does not contain the háčeks and čárkas of standard Czech—and because Czech in Texas today is a spoken and rarely written language—appropriate diacritical notation has fallen out of use within certain contexts, such as Czech-derived place names. On the other hand, actual texts from Texas Czech–language newspapers or other publications usually do have diacritical marks according to standard Czech, and in these cases I've reproduced the passages according to standard usage. Therefore, though a native Czech language speaker might perceive some Czech language portions of the following text as incorrectly written, he or she must bear in mind the Texas-Czech context, with its linguistically unique characteristics, from which they originate.

One final note: throughout the following text, I use the term *Texas Czech* rather than the more accurate *Texas Czech-Moravian* simply to avoid the awkwardness of ponderous repetition. The reader should note that a majority of immigrants to Texas from the Czech lands came from northeastern Moravia, a fact whose effect on modern Texas-Czech culture is still evident.

The map on the following page is an approximation of first- and second-generation Czech-Moravian settlements in Texas. It is meant to show the peak of Czech settlement in a given area and does not necessarily reflect today's Texas-Czech communities.

Sources for the map include Josef Hessoun, *Krátké Dějiny a Seznam Česko-Katolických Osad ve Spoj. Státech Amerických;* Morris, *History of the SPJST;* Christian Sisters, *Unity of the Brethren;* KJT, *Centennial Celebration;* Hudson and Maresh, *Czech Pioneers;* L. W. Jelinek, *Map of Lavaca Co.; Fayette County Courthouse and Communities;* Terry Jordan, *Population Origin Groups in Rural Texas;* Texas A&M University Cartographics Laboratory, *The Roads of Texas;* Machann and Mendl, *Krasna Amerika;* Svrcek, *History;* Národní Svaz Českých Katolíků v Texas, *Naše Dějiny.* Other sources include countless interviews with local historians, fraternal representatives, cotton gin operators, seed store clerks, pensioners, bartenders, barflies, and other local residents. My method was to show subjects a county map and ask them to

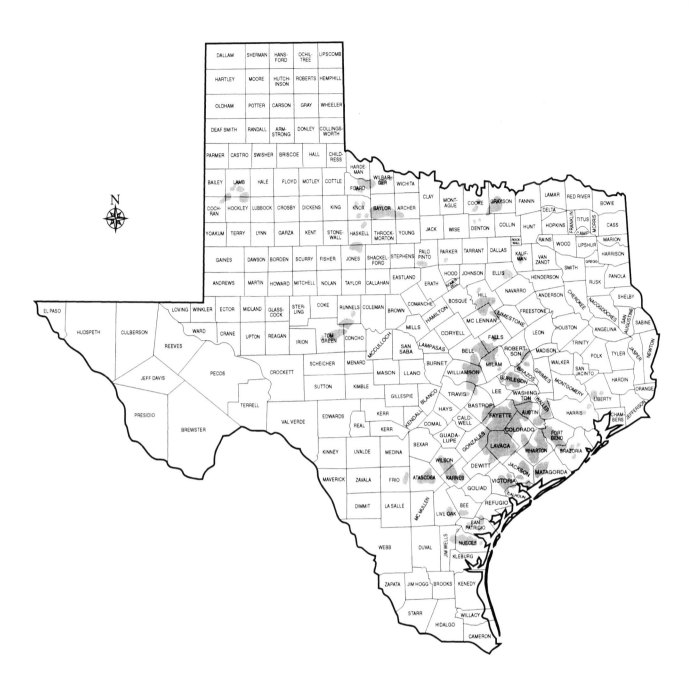

point out specifically where they knew Czechs had once lived and where Czechs had never lived, and also to estimate the peak Czech percentage of the total population in a given area. Often I had to weigh the accuracy of their response by my own instincts; I found subjects who named specific families as they pointed to the map much more reliable than those who replied with general and vague answers. Also, Anglos often had trouble differentiating between Texas Czechs and Germans. Of all the subjects, local Texas-Czech fraternal representatives were the most helpful.

In addition to the areas I indicate, there were Czech settlements at Hermleigh in Scurry County; between Crockett and Lovelady in Houston County; at Beeville in Bee County; at Westhoff, Yorktown, Kubala, and Frydlant in DeWitt County; between Oak Forest and Saint James in Gonzales County; at Brownsville and Rio Hondo in Cameron County; at Edinburg and Mercedes in Hidalgo County; at Millican in Brazos County; at Deweyville in Newton County; and at Saint Lawrence in Glasscock County, among others.

Acknowledgments

First and foremost I would like to thank the hundreds of people I interviewed and photographed for this project. I was constantly amazed at how open you were, how willing you were to let a total stranger with a camera and endless questions into your lives. Thank you.

I also owe my sincerest gratitude to the Texas Chair in Czech Studies at the University of Texas at Austin, without whose generous grants neither the field work nor the publication of this project would have been possible. Thanks as well go to the Czech Ex-Students Association of Texas for their contribution to the funding of this work, and to Dr. Václav Mikušek at the Wallachian Open-Air Museum in Rožnov pod Radhoštěm, Czech Republic.

In addition, special thanks go to J. B. Colson, Bill Stott, Dr. Michael Katz, Thadious Polasek, Dr. Jiří Langer, Victor Peter, Caroline Meiners, Calvin Chervenka, Zigy Kaluzny, Bob Gilka, Gail Fisher, Dr. Ivan Muchka, Kathleen Murphy, Kevin Hannan, and Buddy Polansky.

Part 1

Early History
of Czech Immigration
and Settlement

*Emigration has always involved a complex of dreams, frustrations, false-
hoods, might-have-beens, adventures and blind faith.*

—*Mark Wyman*
Immigrants in the Valley:
Irish, Germans and Americans
in the Upper Mississippi Country,
1830–1860

The Promise of New Opportunity

Though reasons for Czech emigration to Texas varied according to the personal story of the individual émigré, the principal motivation was economic. The Czech lands of Bohemia, Moravia, and Silesia in the nineteenth century formed part of the Austro-Hungarian Empire, whose system of rule favored a German-speaking nobility that exploited the largely Czech-speaking peasantry. While other European nations underwent significant political and social change, the Austro-Hungarian monarchy lagged behind, abolishing feudalism only in 1848. Poor harvests in the mid 1840s, which only marginally improved later on, nearly starved many Czechs, and rapid industrialization in the ensuing years further contributed to the exploitation of this largely disenfranchised people.

Other factors also contributed to the exodus from the homeland. War, such as the one with Prussia in 1866, brought its measure of hardship. Conscription into the Austrian army was a certainty for any able-bodied Czech male at the time. And for Czech-Moravian Brethren, descendants of the Protestant Hussites, religious oppression under the Catholic Hapsburgs created added hardship.

These factors left many Czechs with little hope for an improved standard of living, and many began to consider leaving the homeland behind. In 1856, Konstantin Chovanec, of the little village of Trojanovice in Moravia, made his appeal for emigration:

> *To the Highly Respected Imperial and Royal District Executive!*
>
> *Although I try very hard and work day and night to earn a living for my family and myself, I am hardly able to get enough money to buy salt for the household . . . I slave day and night all week, during which I have 14 hours of sleep all together. . . . For more than four years the crops have been so poor that I have been forced to borrow money at a high rate of interest. . . . I just do not have enough time to describe the poverty and penury of this region, I only dare mention that it would beat anyone with any feeling to go inside some of the cottages.[1]*

It would take several years for Chovanec and eleven others to finally get permission to leave, though the Austrian government eventually saw emigration as an easy and profitable way to relieve its society of potential revolutionary malcontents. A new law in 1866 simplified the application process. Mr. Chovanec finally settled in Fayetteville, Texas.[2]

The momentum of emigration grew rapidly, and America became the primary destination for most of those seeking life elsewhere. In Chovanec's Trojanovice, the population fell from approximately 2,600 in 1857 to 2,030 by 1890. This population drop of 22 percent is almost entirely accounted for by emigrants, 90 percent of whom were destined for Texas. Emigration from Trojanovice continued until 1914.[3]

But why Texas? The state was hardly the only destination of emigrating Czechs—many also left for other parts of the United States, most notably Chicago and the Midwest states, as well as Canada, Brazil, New Zealand, Australia, Russia, and Hungary. Yet for certain Czechs, Texas became the destination of choice, mainly because those who had emigrated before them would write letters back to Europe describing their lives in the New World. Among the first to leave was a Protestant minister named Arnošt Bergman,[4] who, after settling in Austin County at Cat Spring in 1850, began to farm and accumulate land, a luxury inaccessible to many Czechs who had stayed behind. Bergman wrote to his friends describing the opportunity he had found. Encouraged by him, others followed, among them Josef Lešikar, whose subsequent letters from Texas were published in the Moravian newspaper, *Moravské Noviny*.[5] In the area around Čermná in northeastern Bohemia where Bergman and Lešikar were from, talk spread quickly about the new land of opportunity called Texas. The situation in northeastern Moravia was similar, and immigrants to Texas tended to convince others from their home to follow.

Emigration soon became a thriving business, and agents from Bremen and Hamburg, where most of the Czechs boarded ships to cross the Atlantic, advertised in Czech newspapers. Those who left usually had to sell most of their belongings to pay for the trip, though as the Czech population in Texas grew, many new departees left with pre-paid tickets from friends or relatives already in Texas.[6]

The early immigrants faced particularly grueling journeys, for they were easily exploited by profiteering shipping agents, who packed them into ships not equipped to deal with large numbers of passengers. In the 1850s and early 1860s, many died from disease, and those lucky enough to arrive alive in Galveston faced another difficult and often perilous journey inland. Even after the Civil War, when traveling conditions began to improve greatly, conditions were still rough. Rose Urban of Smithville, Texas, born at Kobylí in southern Moravia in 1902, remembers her journey to Texas in 1907: "We were 28 days on a boat and there was a terrible storm, the people were crying and throwing up. It was awfully hard on mama 'cause she was pregnant." Mrs. Urban, unlike most Czechs who came to Texas, arrived via New York. She still remembers the Statue of Liberty: "I saw the lady standing there—I didn't know what it meant, but I cheered."[7]

The Czech population in Texas stood at approximately seven hundred by the time of the Civil War,[8] when virtually all immigration ceased with the Union blockade of Texas ports. After the war's end, immigration returned with full speed, and the period of 1870 to 1920 represents the height of Czech emigration to Texas. Approximately 90 percent of immigrants came from the area around Lanškroun in Bohemia and from three areas in Moravia: around Vsetín, Zádveřice, and Frenštát pod Radhoštěm.[9] Robert Janak, in his pioneering study of Texas-Czech tombstone inscriptions, found the following distribution of geographic origin by birth:

40.8% *from Lachia (northeastern Moravia, including Frenštát);*

40.2% *from Wallachia (also northeastern Moravia, south of Lachia, including Vsetín and Zádveřice);*

9.9% *from Lanškroun (northeastern Bohemia);*

2.4% *from southern Bohemia; and*

6.7% *unidentified or from other areas.*[10]

Janak's figures show that at least 81 percent of the immigrants in his study came from northeastern Moravia, a fact that would have a considerable effect on Texas-Czech culture and language to the present day.

Records kept by immigration authorities do not track internal U.S. settlement, so how many Czech immigrants actually came to Texas is extremely difficult to ascertain. Also, pre-1918 records include Bohemia and Austria among lands of origin but not Moravia. And even if they did, the records would still not be conclusive because not all emigrants from the Czech lands were Czech; some ethnic Germans who came to Texas came from Bohemia and Moravia, and some ethnic Czechs in Texas came from other nations, such as Russia, Germany, and Switzerland.

Somewhat more helpful are state census figures, which for 1920 show a total of 14,871 foreign-born Czech-language speakers,[11] though this figure does not indicate the number of Czech immigrants who had already died or left Texas. The same census also shows 49,929 first- and second-generation Czechs, identified by the language spoken in the country of origin of one or both parents. And the census of 1940 reveals a total of 62,680 Texans whose first language was Czech.[12] Czech immigration to Texas dwindled by 1920. By then the first Czechoslovak Republic had been established, and much of the impetus for people to leave had subsided.[13]

The U.S. Civil War had a greater effect on Czechs in Texas than halting the flow of emigration from the motherland. Though some joined one or the other side, for the most part Czechs had little desire to fight in someone else's war. Military conscription, after all, was what had convinced many to leave Europe in the first place. Also, with their firm religious convictions, most Czechs did not agree with slavery, and so saw little reason to fight for a state that did.[14] Instead, many Czechs either hid from the Confederate officers seeking enlistees or joined the teamsters hauling cotton to Mexico. Being a teamster excluded them from military service because the sale of cotton was crucial to the survival of the Confederate army.[15] But whether they fought in the war or hauled cotton across the border, the newly arrived Czech pioneer family suffered extreme hardship because of its dependence on the able-bodied males of the household. Their absence also made the families easier prey for marauding bandits.[16]

Yet perhaps even more significant is the effect the Civil War had on the Czech immigrants' relationship with Anglo Americans. Czechs arrived in Texas already feeling estranged, for few could speak English and all were unaccustomed to many of the ways of their Anglo neighbors. The war highlighted differences between Czechs and Anglos, causing resentment on both sides. And though the arriving Czechs were by nature clannish in their social relations, the war no doubt reinforced their sense of otherness, a sense that they must stick together in this new and foreign land. Ironically, though the Czechs had come to Texas in part to flee their German-speaking rulers, the Civil War pushed Germans and Czechs in Texas together—both shared similar attitudes toward the war, and both bore the punishment of not wanting to participate.[17]

Early Settlement in Texas

Czechs arrived in Texas relatively late in the European emigration of the nineteenth century; Germans in particular had already settled much of the land in the areas of early Czech settlement. The Czechs arriving at Cat Spring in the 1850s found that much of the land was already taken, so they began to spread outward, buying acreage at nearby New Ulm, New Bremen, and Frelsburg. Further arrivees pushed west into Fayette County, around Fayetteville in 1853[18] and Hostyn in 1856,[19] the latter becoming the first substantial Czech settlement in Texas. Partly due to the efforts of F. J. Spacek, an immigrant entrepreneur who helped fellow Czechs find housing and farms, Fayetteville and its surrounding communities of Ross Prairie, Rek Hill, and Bordovice attracted Czech settlers. Fayetteville, originally an Anglo settlement founded in 1833 and later settled heavily by Germans, became predominantly Czech by the 1880s, and today is recognized by many as "the cradle of Czech settlement" in Texas.[20] Other Czech settlements established in the 1850s include Dubina, Ammannsville, and Praha in Fayette County, Novohrad in Lavaca County, and Veseli (now Wesley) in Washington County.[21]

Two factors probably more than any others dictated the direction of Czech settlement in Texas: the price and quality of land. The Czechs favored blackland prairie, a rich soil ideal for raising crops that runs in two swathes through Texas: a smaller one beginning in Gonzales and Lavaca counties, going northeast, and petering out around Brazos and Grimes counties; the second and much larger one running from around San

Antonio in Bexar County all the way north to Grayson and other counties bordering Oklahoma.[22]

In order to follow the initial growth and spread of Czech settlements in Texas, one need only follow the blackland prairie: from Fayette County up into Burleson and Brazos counties, where Czechs settled at Caldwell, Snook, Frenstat, Hranice, Lyons, New Tabor, Tabor, Kurten, and Wheelock. Significant Czech settlements that follow the second tract of blackland prairie begin around Smithville and Kovar in Bastrop County, then pick up again around Rice's Crossing, Taylor, Granger, and Jarrell in Williamson County; around Cameron, Buckholts, Rogers, Cyclone, Ratibor, and Seaton in Milam and Bell counties; then farther north at Mart, Elk, Tours, West, Abbott, and Penelope in McLennan and Hill counties; at Ennis, Bardwell, Alma, Crisp, Telico, and Palmer in Ellis County; at Kaufman and Terrel near Dallas in Kaufman County; and finally finishing at Pilot Point, Tioga, Gunter, and Southmayd in Denton and Grayson counties.

The demand for land was great, however, and the new Czech settlers ventured into new areas wherever they saw promise. Most continued to filter through the mother colonies in Fayette County and vicinity, then traveled on upon hearing of land offers they could afford. Around 1880, for instance, Czechs began arriving in Nada in southern Colorado County and in 1900 in East Bernard in nearby Wharton County.[23] These settlement trends continued, and within only a few years both counties, as well as Fort Bend County, had heavy Czech settlements, at El Campo, Louise, Wharton, Needville, Rosenberg, Guy, Hillje, Hungerford, and Ganado in Jackson County. From here they pushed farther south toward Victoria, with settlements at Kopecky Town, Blessing, Lolita, Marekville, Shillerville, La Salle, Inez, Holub, and Placedo.

Often the patterns of settlement were circuitous. Some Czechs who settled initially around Corpus Christi, at places like the Bohemia Colony Settlement, Robstown, Agua Dulce, Alice, Orange Grove, Sinton, Taft, Skidmore, and Olmos—which are all farther south than the settlements around El Campo—came not from the Fayette area, but much farther north, from Taylor, Granger, and West.[24] Czechs from these latter areas also

headed into Central Texas to buy farmland around San Angelo and Rowena. They also settled at Bohemia, Miles, and Wall, while fellow compatriots established significant North Texas settlements at Megargel, Bomarton, Seymour, Thalia, and Vernon, and even as far north as Anton and Littlefield in the southern Panhandle.[25]

Also worthy of mention are the Czechs who worked in the coal mines at Thurber and Lyra, some of whom, when coal production there ceased in 1921, were among the Czechs who settled the mines around Crockett and Lovelady in East Texas.[26]

Community Structure

Of the values the Czechs brought with them to Texas, perhaps three more than any others dictated the structure and growth of their communities: religion, education, and fraternalism. Most Czechs coming to Texas were of a single social class known as *chalupníci*, or cottagers: people who owned a small house and sometimes a small amount of land.[27] These were people who placed great value in hard work and manual labor and had little regard for class hierarchy. In Texas this translated to Czech communities that were socially very stable with minimal class stratification. Community members often worked together for common goals: the construction of churches and schools and the creation of mutual aid societies were of top priority.

One of the first concerns of the typical emerging Czech community in Texas was the fulfillment of its religious needs. For both Czech Catholics and Protestant Brethren, Czech-speaking priests and pastors were greatly appreciated and in scarce supply. The first Czech priest in Texas, Father Josef Chromčík, arrived on Christmas Eve in 1872 in Fayetteville, where he stayed to organize his local parish and to build a school. Word spread of his arrival, and within several years Chromčík was saying mass at Czech settlements in Fayette, Austin, Lavaca, Burleson, Washington, Williamson, Ellis, and McLennan counties, covering the distance of several hundred miles on horseback.[28]

Just as the Czech settlers needed a spiritual leader, they also needed a church in which to meet and hear his message, and despite very limited resources, community members often joined together to build one. The Czech churches in Texas vary greatly in size and style, and often reflect the size and vitality of the parish. Usually the first church built was small and plain, and as the local population grew, parishioners built larger churches to accommodate new members (the replacement of churches was often a necessity due to their vulnerability to tornadoes and fire). Many, like the Catholic churches at Fayetteville, Hostyn, Holman, Praha, Ammannsville, High Hill, Dubina, Wallis, Shiner, Corn Hill, Sweet Home, and Weimar, were truly spectacular architecturally, and one can only wonder at the sincerity and dedication of the parishioners who built them. Unfortunately, the first three of these original structures no longer exist.

Early Czech settlers arrived with a historically strong tradition of elementary education, and the construction of a school to educate their children was as important as the church to maintain their souls. And because so many immigrants arrived with no knowledge of English, teachers in the first schools taught primarily in Czech, first at Wesley (Veseli) in 1859.[29] Settlements at Velehrad, Novohrad, Vysehrad, Ross Prairie, and Bila Hora also had Czech-language schools.[30] The journalist Ludvík Dongres in 1924 notes that native language instruction struck an emotional note with the Czechs: they "felt that it is a duty to maintain their national identity by preserving their language, and so they have not wanted to send their children to English-language schools."[31]

In 1871, however, the Texas Legislature passed a law that all headmasters pass an English proficiency test and that English be used as the primary language of instruction. The Czech community eventually agreed, though only after very heated debate and delayed implementation in some areas. Local parishes were also very involved in education, and by 1924, Texas had seventy-seven Czech Catholic parochial schools, more than any state in the country. Czech interest in maintaining the instruction of their language remained strong, and they organized several societies whose aim was to provide funding.[32]

Most early Czech schools were one-room school houses with one or two instructors, the funding for which came from community residents. Teaching resources were limited (many did not even have textbooks), and most schools only went to the fifth or sixth grade. Because children were also very involved in the labor required at the family farm, Czechs in nineteenth-century Texas on the whole did not emphasize higher education.[33]

In order to better cope with the difficulties of starting over in a new land with few resources, Czech immigrants established fraternal societies to provide different forms of mutual aid. The largest and most important of these were insurance companies, some of which, like the *Rolnický Vzájemný Ochranný Spolek Státu Texas* or RVOS (Farmer's Mutual Protective Association of Texas), catered to specific occupational groups. Others, like the *Česká Řimsko-Katolická Jednota Texaská* or KJT (Czech Catholic Union of Texas), sought to provide life insurance based on religious affiliation. Life insurance was especially vital to families in rural areas, who were very dependent on the husband's abilities and labor. Should anything happen to him, the widow and her children (six to ten children were not uncommon) would be left in a precarious situation. These fraternal organizations operated with local chapters and lodges that also functioned as venues for other purposes, for everything from chamber of commerce meetings to polka dances, and hence provided important centers of local activity that strengthened the stability of the Czech communities.

The concept of fraternalism did not stop with insurance. Clubs and organizations sprang up everywhere to serve the needs of the community. Cooperative stores and cotton gins provided much needed credit to poor farmers. Reading clubs accumulated small libraries of Czech literature in a state where any Czech text was hard to find. Beef clubs ensured a steady supply of fresh meat at a time when the most common form of refrigeration was the bottom of a well. Sokol, the Prague-based nineteenth-century gymnastics organization whose purpose was to instill physical stamina and Czech national awareness, trained the newer generations at chapters across the state. Other organizations were based on philanthropic causes, like the Dallas Circle of

Czech Women, which raised money for charitable events, and the Czech Ex-Students Association of Texas, which provided scholarship money for university education. What is important about all these organizations is that they not only provided a social network and economic cushion for new immigrants, but most, being founded *by* Czechs *for* Czechs, helped maintain the integrity of Texas-Czech culture.

Organizations like the fraternal societies were important in keeping alive a sense of ethnic solidarity for Czech communities scattered across the state, a role the emerging Czech-language press, both newspapers and radio, helped to fulfill as well. The first Czech newspaper in Texas was the weekly *Texan,* changed later to *Slovan* and published in La Grange until 1890. Two other publications founded in the nineteenth century, the Catholic weekly *Nový Domov* (*New Home*) from Hallettsville and weekly *Svoboda* (*Freedom*) from La Grange and later El Campo, were probably the most influential. Both continued publication until the 1960s. In all, Texas has had at least thirty-four Czech-language publications,[34] two of which, *Hospodář* and *Našinec,* still exist. These publications catered to the interests of their readers, providing news from the many Czech communities and advice on farming practices. They also provided information on national, state, and local issues, which allowed Czechs to participate successfully in the democratic process.[35] Local radio also became an important medium for cultural preservation, broadcasting local news and Czech music across the state.

Everyday Life

The average Czech family in turn-of-the-century Texas lived on a farm, and every able-bodied family member participated in maintaining it. Whether that meant picking cotton or shucking corn, curing bacon or cooking dinner, all duties were crucial in a system that allotted equal importance to farmstead and household. The guiding influence behind the performance of these actions and many other aspects of Czech life in Texas was a concept known as *hospodářství,* which in English translates to the archaic word "husbandry." The fundamental meaning of *hospodářství* boils down to the fru-

gal use of money and other resources combined with pride in the execution of duties both great and small. The concept has not only been a central value within Texas-Czech culture, but has also contributed to the survival of those employing it. In the fields this meant not just healthy ears of corn, but rows planted neatly and evenly spaced and weeds methodically removed. Material things were meant to last—to be repaired at home and kept from showing excessive wear, and not to be discarded according to fashion. *Hospodářství* also promoted a strong tendency toward self-sufficiency; every farm included not only the crops that would be sold for money, but large gardens with fruits and vegetables, coops full of hens, geese, and guineas, and a few acres for hogs and several head of cattle. Though eggs might be bartered at the local cooperative store, most of what the average Czech family produced stayed at home to be consumed or shared with friends and relatives.[36] *Hospodářství* also formed the basis by which people judged each others' actions, and a lack of *hospodářství* was a much more serious fault than getting drunk in public or not showing up for church.[37]

As a consequence of both *hospodářství* and their mostly agrarian economy, Czechs in Texas developed a strong bond with the land. After all, land ownership had been out of reach for many in the mother country, and the vast stretches of rich, virgin prairie in Texas were perhaps the greatest symbol that enticed them to explore new opportunity. Land ownership, therefore, became an important indicator of status and success, as well as a practical asset.[38] Even nonfarming Czechs often had a few acres in order to keep a vegetable patch and some livestock. The importance of land ownership undoubtedly also slowed the Czechs' rate of assimilation and loss of original ethnic identity; America's land, rather than American society, became their gateway to new opportunity and a new life.

The Czechs brought with them a strong emphasis on family and family ties, something reinforced in Texas by the requirements of living off the land. Families tended to be large, and children often lived at home even through the first years of married life. Once they set off on their own, many (until World War II) stayed within the community, following pursuits similar to those of their parents. A husband and wife usually shared equally in making family decisions, and though their roles within the household were different, the labor of both was vital to the family's survival.[39] Consequently the network of family relations within a particular settlement was strong, which, together with their strong ethnic identity, made many Czech communities seem clannish and introverted to outsiders.

Social life revolved around the family and the community, with picnics, weddings, polka dances, and church bazaars bringing the scattered settlers together. Music especially became a vital asset in the social life of all the Czech settlements, most of which had their own family orchestras that played traditional Czech polka and waltz music at any celebratory occasion. Local bars, beer joints, and fraternal lodges became important places for community members to relax and share gossip over a game of dominoes or *taroks,* a card game the Czechs brought with them to Texas and still play today.

Assimilation v. Ethnic Preservation

The Czechs that came to Texas sought for the most part to become true citizens of their new homeland. Texas Czechs fought bravely in the two world wars and most became U.S. citizens. They participated in local politics (most voted Democratic), electing fellow Texas Czechs to public office across the state. Probably the most influential leader ever within the Texas-Czech community was Augustin Haidusek, who served two terms in the Texas Legislature and also founded *Svoboda.* He argued vociferously that his compatriots accept the responsibilities of American citizenship—particularly in the debate over English v. Czech as the primary language of elementary school instruction—and his push for assimilation won a majority of support within the Texas-Czech community.[40]

At the same time, Texas Czechs sought to preserve their ethnicity, their culture, and their way of life, a practice that created near-cultural islands out of many Texas-Czech settlements. In his account of growing up in the Czech–Moravian Brethren community of Snook, Robert Skrabanek describes a strong sense of otherness from "Americans," brought on by the impression that Czechs simply worked harder and did things better than their Anglo neighbors.[41] Pride rather than arrogance was the defining feature of the average Texas Czechs in regard to their ethnic identity, a pride whose roots lay perhaps in the attempted suppression of their culture by the Austrians in the nineteenth century. In any case, though the Czechs accepted America as their new home, they structured their communities and their lives according to their own ways. From the newspapers they read to the language they preferred, from the organizations they joined to the values they espoused, their Czech-Moravian origin was reflected throughout.

Clinton Machann and James Mendl describe World War II as the "end of an era" in the Czech-Moravian communities of Texas. Their culturally fortified settlements proved no match for the social and technological changes brought on by the war and its aftermath.[42] A host of complex factors came together to unravel the cohesion within the Texas-Czech community, and both Czech culture and language declined dramatically. The war pulled young Texas-Czech men from their rural and often isolated communities and exposed them to mainstream America, and many of those who returned had little desire to maintain the ethnic identity of their parents. In 1948, the communists took power in Czechoslovakia, leading in many cases to personal ties being severed with the old country. As McCarthyism blossomed, so did the pressure to relinquish association with a country officially in the enemy's camp. Even at home the context that had allowed the Czechs their cultural independence changed: the completion of the state highway system began to break down the isolation of their settlements, and changes within the economic structure of the country lured the newest generation away to the big cities. By the early 1950s, though many Texas-Czech children were still growing up with little use for English, television and a strengthened public school system quickly replaced their language of choice.

The Experience of Rozie Belicek

Though many Texas Czechs found the opportunity that had been unavailable to them in Bohemia and Moravia, the lives of most offered hard work and meager reward.

Many arrived without enough money to buy land, so they got jobs wherever they could, and this often meant living as a sharecropper picking cotton. Until the post–World War II period, cotton was truly king, and harvesting it before the advent of the mechanized cotton-picker was grueling work. In her memoirs Rozie Belicek, who came to Texas as a young mother in 1908, wrote: "Gladly looking towards August when there will be cotton to pick; that this will be an easier American work. We were mistaken. The August American sun burned our backs, and it took so long to fill those long sacks, and with my fingers all pricked and bloody. I barely picked 100 pounds a day. We were paid 50 cents for 100 pounds. My husband was worse off for he barely picked 50 pounds."[43]

Eventually the Beliceks rented land by working halves, which meant that the landowner would provide them with housing, seed, implements, and horses, and in return he would receive half of the harvested crop. Yet this did not mark the beginning of a much-improved life. Landowners (often fellow Czechs) exploited them and had little sympathy for their poverty. On top of it all, nature seldom cooperated. Mrs. Belicek writes of frost, hurricanes, ruined crops, and Spanish flu, and with her family growing, she and her husband eventually moved across the state in search of better conditions: from Bryan south to Veseli and Industry, then north to Tioga near Oklahoma, then south again to the Lavaca County area—Smithville, Moravia, Hackberry, Schulenburg, and Moulton, then south again to Lolita and finally Ganado, where they bought land in the 1930s.

Not long before her death she wrote: "Today in my 87 years in ill health following a stroke, I am looking back on my whole life which was full of hardship; that constant struggle for mere existence. I often wonder how it was possible to endure and live through it all: always having courage to fight over and over again life destiny [*sic*]. My efforts were to insure and take care of our family welfare under conditions, of which the present generation cannot even imagine."[44]

Notes

1. Drahomír Strnadel et al., *Tam za mořem je Amerika*, p. 5.
2. V. A. Svrcek, *A History of the Czech-Moravian Catholic Communities of Texas*, p. 70.
3. Drahomír Strnadel, interview by author, Trojanovice, Czech Republic, July 8, 1994.
4. Clinton Machann and James Mendl mention that Father Bohumir Menzl arrived with "a few Czech families" in 1840 and settled among the Germans at New Braunfels and Fredericksburg. The first Czech in Texas was probably Karel Anton Postl in 1823 (see Machann and Mendl, *Krasna Amerika: A Study of the Texas Czechs, 1851–1939*, p. 22).
5. Ibid., p. 28.
6. Ibid., p. 20.
7. Rose Urban, interview by author, Smithville, Texas, Feb. 24, 1994.
8. Machann and Mendl, *Krasna Amerika*, p. 35.
9. Edmond Hejl, *Czechs and Moravians in Texas*.
10. Robert Janak, *Geographic Origins of Czech Texas*.
11. U.S. Bureau of the Census, *Fourteenth Census of the United States: 1920, Volume 2, General Report and Analytical Tables* (Washington: U.S. Government Printing Office, 1923), table 10, p. 1001.
12. U.S. Bureau of the Census, *Sixteenth Census of the United States: 1940, Nativity and Parentage of the White Population: Mother Tongue*, (Washington: U.S. Government Printing Office, 1943), p. 978.
13. Machann and Mendl, *Krasna Amerika*, p. 67.
14. See the account of Jan Horák in Clinton Machann and James Mendl, eds., *Czech Voices*, p. 78–83.
15. Jody Feldtman Wright, *Czechs in Grey and Blue, Too!*
16. Machann and Mendl, *Krasna Amerika*, p. 38. For more information on the experience of Texas Czechs in the Civil War, see Wright's *Czechs in Grey and Blue, Too!* and the accounts of František Branecký and Jan Ustyník in Machann and Mendl, *Czech Voices*.
17. For further information on Germans in Texas, see G. G. Benjamin, *The Germans in Texas: A Study of Immigration*; R. L. Biesele, *The History of the German Settlements in Texas, 1831–1861*; F. Roemer, *Texas; with particular reference to German immigration and the physical appearance of the country*; Vera Flach, *A Yankee in German-America*; Goethe-Institut, *Lone Star & Eagle: German Immigration to Texas*; and L. Goodwin,
W. Watriss, and F. Baldwin, *Coming to Terms: The German Hill Country of Texas*.
18. Svrcek, *History*, p. 70.
19. Czech Catholic Union of Texas (KJT), *The Czech Catholic Union of Texas Centennial Celebration*.
20. Robert Zelade, "Room to Grow," *Texas Highways* (Sept. 1993): 56.
21. Machann and Mendl, *Krasna Amerika*, p. 35.
22. See map in the University of Texas at Austin's Bureau of Business Research's *Atlas of Texas*, p. 12.
23. Svrcek, *History*.
24. Ibid.
25. Ibid.
26. Bessie Striz, interview by author, Strawn, Texas, May 3, 1994.
27. Machann and Mendl, *Krasna Amerika*, chaps. 1 and 3.
28. KJT, *Centennial Celebration*.
29. From a display about the Wesley (Veseli) settlement at the Burleson County Czech Heritage Museum, Caldwell, Texas.
30. Connie Sherwood Smith, "The Demise of Czech in Two Texas Communities" (Ph.D. diss., the University of Texas at Austin, 1991) and Machann and Mendl, *Krasna Amerika*.
31. See Machann and Mendl, *Czech Voices*, p. 128. See also L. W. Dongres's detailed account of the establishment of early schools in "Paměti starých českých osadníků v Americe." In *Amerikán Národni Kalendař* (Chicago: Nakl. Ing. Geringera, 1924), pp. 124–27.
32. Machann and Mendl, *Krasna Amerika*, chap. 3.
33. Ibid.
34. Machann and Mendl, *Krasna Amerika*, pp. 272–73, list 33. Additionally, the socialist *Pozor* published from 1910 to 1916 in Hallettsville (see Paul Boethel, *History of Lavaca County*).
35. Kevin Hannan, "A Study of the Culture of the Czech Moravian Community in Texas," unpublished manuscript, 1985.
36. For further insight into the life of an early Czech family in Texas, see Robert L. Skrabanek, *We're Czechs*.
37. Machann and Mendl, *Krasna Amerika*, p. 82.
38. Ibid., chap. 3.
39. Ibid. and Skrabanek, *We're Czechs*.
40. For further information on Augustin Haidusek, see Machann and Mendl, *Krasna Amerika*, pp. 221–27; William P. Hewitt, ed., *The Czech Texans*; Estelle Hudson

and Henry Maresh, *Czech Pioneers of the Southwest;* and Jesse Jochec, "The Life and Career of Augustin Haidusek" (master's thesis, the University of Texas at Austin, 1940).

41. See Skrabanek, *We're Czechs,* preface.

42. Machann and Mendl, *Krasna Amerika,* p. 2.

43. See Rozie Belicek, "The Story of My Life, Part 2: For a Better Future Across the Ocean," unpublished manuscript, 1972, p. 2.

44. Ibid., p. 8.

Part 2

Journeys

Frank J. Spacek was thirteen when, in 1866, he left his village of Bordovice in Moravia to come to Fayetteville. In 1931, he wrote in his memoirs:

> *V roku 1868 v měsíci červnu p. Walla přijel s města a přinesl mí psaní s Evropy; já ale neměl tolik času psaní přečisti. Musel jsem rychle vsednout na koně a ujíždět pro voly asi čtyry míle na prerie, tam kde jest ted' osada tak zvaná Lone Star; netrvalo to dlouho když jsem přijel na místo, brzy jsem voly našel. Ted' jsem se posadil, psaní otevřel a začnu číst. Tu vidím otec mi píše: 'Milý synu, zde ti píšem smutnou novinu, tvá milá maminka zemřela, již ji vidět ne nebudeš.' Ten okamžik nikdy nezapomenu, jak mne lítost projela, já se lítosti po prerii válel a plakal* [sic].

(In June of 1868 Mr. Walla came from town and brought me a letter from Europe, though I had no time to read it. Immediately I had to ride my horse four miles to get the oxen that were on the prairie, near today's settlement of Lone Star; it didn't take long to get there and I soon found the oxen. Then I sat down, opened the letter and began to read. It was from my father: "Dear son, I am writing you sad news. Your sweet mother has died, never again will you see her." I will never forget that moment, how my sorrow passed through me. In my grief I rolled over on the prairie and wept.)[1]

The Czech settlers arriving in turn-of-the-century Texas established initial colonies in Fayette and Lavaca counties, such as at Bila Hora (above). Driven by the search for good farming land at a price they could afford, the Czechs fanned out across the state and established pockets of settlement, including at Megargel in Archer County (opposite page, below).

In 1885, Jan Halamiček founded the settlement of Roznov in Fayette County, naming it after his birthplace of Rožnov pod Radhoštěm in Moravia. The Texas town prospered with a cotton gin, school, blacksmith, and Halamiček's general store-saloon. "We used to get more people on the weekend than Fayetteville," says son Ben, eighty-six, standing in front of the Roznov house where he grew up (opposite page, above). By the 1920s, though, Roznov had begun to decline. In the 1930s, because of competition from businesses in nearby towns, Ben closed the store he had taken over from his father. "They'd have some specials, but them other things, they were more expensive," he says.

Born in Slovakia, Father John Hanacek came to Texas as a boy with
his father in 1919 to join Moravian relatives who had settled around
La Grange. "My Daddy was afraid there'd be more war in Europe, so
we had to leave. . . . When we got here I remember my relatives had
a long table laid out with all kinds of food—we couldn't figure out
how there could be so much. I thought I was in Heaven!" he says.
Father Hanacek grew up farming cotton and corn with his parents,
and after attending seminary school, he returned to serve the Catholic
parishes in Fayette and Lavaca counties, including, since 1977, Saint
John the Baptist Church at Ammannsville (above).

Many Czechs arrived in Texas with names that were difficult for non-Czechs to remember and often impossible to pronounce. And though the Czech immigrants by and large maintained a strong desire to preserve their ethnic identity, they also wanted to participate in American society. Names like Svrcek, Crnkovic, and Hrncir seemed a hindrance to assimilation, leading some people to change the spelling of their name, as from Hrncir to Hencher, or even to change their name entirely. One woman told me about a Kovar who changed his name to Smith, so strong was his desire to embrace the ways of the New World.

Lorain Deem is anxious to record the songs of her youth sung by her parents, Rose and August Konvicka. "Some of them are sad, others made us smile, but they're all so beautiful," she says—songs like "Už mě žáden, nemá rád" and "Vidím *ptáčka* v černém lese." Her parents can recite nearly two hundred songs, some Czech, some Moravian, some written in Texas, and all of which they learned growing up in the village of Moravia in Lavaca County. Even today after the first few verses of "Hřbitove, hřbitove," Lorain and her sister, Linda, still break into tears.

Angelina Bednar, eighty, still remembers when the area near Latium in Washington County was called Ujetov, the Czech people's way of saying Hewitt's Place. The Czechs came in the 1870s and farmed for Mr. Hewitt, who owned much of the land there at the time. They established a little Catholic parish, and even heard Czech-language sermons from the Czech priests sent to them by their bishop. "But then one day the bishop sent us a Polish priest who couldn't talk Czech," says Mrs. Bednar. "And boy my daddy was mad because Daddy couldn't talk any English. So he went to the bishop and asked if we could have a Czech priest, but the bishop said, 'No, you've got to learn English,' so then me and my sisters had to teach Daddy English! But that Polish priest, he learned Czech after not too long."

The early Czechs brought to Texas a cultural tradition rich in folklore, full of stories about *rusalky* (water nymphs), *rarášky* (evil spirits), and *čarodějnice* (witches), all of whom seemed to invariably prey upon disobedient little children. The most commonly recounted of these supernatural evils was the *Vodník,* also called the *Hastrman.* The *Vodník* often has a long white beard, green hair, and webbed feet or claws. He lives in rivers and creeks, and awaits the chance to catch wading boys and girls by the ankle and pull them to his watery keep. Songs, like the following, could keep him away.

> *Hastrmane, tatrmane, vylez z vody ven.*
> *Dej nám kožich na buben.*
> *Budeme ti bubnovati, až vylezeš z vody ven.*[2]

> *(Hastrman, fool, come out of the water.*
> *Give us a hide for a drum*
> *We'll beat on it for you until you come out of the water.)*

Though much of the original Czech-Moravian folk culture has disappeared, some aspects of it still survive. Rita and Leo Janak of Wied in Lavaca County still dress up as Saint Nicholas and the devil every year (opposite page, above) in the few weeks before Christmas and visit local children to find out who's been good. Opposite page, below, a wreath announces "Merry Christmas" in Fayetteville.

Among the original Czech-Moravian cultural forms that have survived in Texas is the *kroj,* the traditional folk costumes that have been passed down through generations (some Texas Czechs now buy costumes in the Czech Republic). The costumes vary greatly in style and color, and identify a specific village of origin. (opposite page, below), Texas women prepare to exhibit their Kyjov *kroje* in a parade of costumes at the Czech Tent at the Texas State Fair.

Homemade Texas versions of the *kroj* are common and sometimes incorporate visual elements to represent Texas, such as the bluebonnets and the state map in the costume of Bill Vornsand of Schulenburg (above). And though Carol Mraz admits she has never seen a Czech meadow, it nevertheless inspired her choice of fabrics for her own Texas-Czech costume (opposite page, above), which she wears once a year at the Ennis Polka Festival. Mraz, who lived in Houston for twenty-seven years, admits that when she returned to live in Ennis she "came back to [her] roots." Such blending of Czech and Texas symbols in the costumes suggest the prevalence of a unique *Texas*-Czech identity.

Family Portrait
The Koreneks of Ellinger

"We still like to do things our own kind of way," says Vlasta Korenek, who with her husband, Lawrence, and two sons, James and Lawrence Jr., lives on their farm just outside of Ellinger. Whether it's butchering their own hogs to make *klobasa* (sausage) and *špek* (bacon), or making *kyška* (clabber) from their cows into *tvaroh* (cottage cheese), the Koreneks, like most of the early Czech settlers in Texas, prefer to do what they can themselves. "The stuff you buy in the stores is so

expensive nowadays, and lots of it isn't even any good," explains Vlasta, who also makes her own soap, bread, and *koláče*.

Though Vlasta and Lawrence Sr. are third-generation Texas Czechs, they and their sons speak a mixture of Czech and English with one another. "Jokes in Czech are just *so* funny, but in English they're just not," says Vlasta of jokes like *Za každým Čechem letí čert s měchem* (Behind every Bohemian flies the devil with a sack). At twenty-seven, James (above, left) is the youngest person in the Ellinger area to speak and read Czech fluently. "There aren't too many young people left who can speak it," he says, "but some of the older people still speak it better than English."

With their father the two sons leave home by 6:30 every morning (above) for their jobs with a local oil well and pipeline repair company, which provides their main source of income. The hogs, cattle, and corn they raise create hard work but little money. "There just ain't no profit in it anymore," says James. "I farm yet because I like it. Some people play basketball or baseball—I don't care none for that."

James and Lawrence Jr. have maintained their Texas-Czech ways largely by resisting the pull to the big cities that has led to the demise

of much of Texas-Czech culture. "People who go to the city think they can make the easy money. They don't want to do any real work," says James. Though the Koreneks have chosen not to join the rural exodus, neither do they isolate themselves. The family is responsible for maintaining the cemetery at nearby Saint Mary's Church, Vlasta and James participate in the church choir, and Lawrence Jr. is treasurer of the local KJT society. "We never got time to even think if something hurts, we're so busy," says Vlasta with a laugh.

"The older people keep dyin' out, and the younger generation don't know how to read the Czech language," says Joe Vrabel, owner, publisher, and editor of *Našinec*, one of two newspapers in Texas that is still published entirely in Czech. Since Czech immigration to Texas began, the state has had at least thirty-four different Czech-language newspapers and periodicals, the biggest of which, *Nový Domov* (*New Home*) and *Svoboda* (*Freedom*), ceased publication in the 1960s.

Vrabel does not seek to inform his readers about news of the world. Rather, *Našinec*, like much of the early Texas-Czech press, functions as a means for the Czech-language readers spread across Texas to maintain a certain solidarity. "I'm trying to pick stuff out you don't hear every day," explains Vrabel, "and I don't do any editorial—I try and stay neutral." News from the scattered Czech communities, recipes, obituaries, reminiscences, and little stories are what fill *Našinec*'s pages.

Našinec's readers are also its writers, and ninety-one-year-old Rose Urban is one of the paper's most loyal reporters. "I like to write something funny," she says, "'cause funerals and all—who wants to read about that all the time?" Though *Našinec* had a circulation of over fifteen hundred when Mr. Vrabel took it over in 1981, by 1993 subscriptions had fallen to about seven-hundred and fifty. "I got a feeling it won't stay around too much longer," he says.

Once every three weeks, Al Steffek and members of eleven other families in the area around Vysehrad in Lavaca County take turns donating a calf to be butchered for their own consumption. Such "beef clubs" were once common among the early immigrants, who lacked adequate refrigeration and would organize themselves into clubs in order to ensure a proper supply of fresh meat. Though Mr. Steffek and the other members have kept in pace with modern technology, they still adhere to the old tradition. "There just ain't nothin' better than beef that hasn't been chilled," says Steffek. "That's what you call *real* beef. I'll take it home and eat it for supper, and I'll eat it for breakfast tomorrow too." Beef club members rotate which part of the calf each will receive according to a diagram, and each piece is weighed and recorded to guarantee fairness.

Though a majority of Texans may know little or nothing about Texas-Czech culture, most know and appreciate kolaches, the small pastries with a fruit, cheese, or poppy seed center. And perhaps nowhere else in the state are so many of the pastries baked in so short a time as at the Unity of the Brethren Church in Taylor, whose members volunteer twice a year to bake kolaches all night long (left). The succeeding shifts prepare approximately six thousand of the little pastries, which will start to sell the following morning. Baking leader Christine Kubala, eighty-two, doesn't worry about leftovers. "In three hours they'll all be gone," she says.

Sausage too is an intrinsic part of the Texas-Czech kitchen, and in Texas-Czech communities across the state, family meat markets prepare a wide variety. At Patek's of Shiner, original recipes have been passed down through generations. (Above), Jimmy Patek and Gilbert Schroeder encase a fresh batch of beef sausage.

"I been playin' about sixty years, all our kids know how to play. I can't win, but I play," says Annie Cernosek (left) of the tarok game she plays once a week at the Farm Bureau building in little Swiss Alp in Fayette County. Taroks (not to be confused with tarot) is likely a legacy of Austrian influence on the early Czechs who came to Texas. Still popular in Texas-Czech communities today, it is uncommon in the modern Czech Republic. The game requires specialized cards (above) and involves Czech-language commands and responses. Texas-Czech fraternals organize local tournaments throughout the year, such as the one sponsored by the Slavonic Benevolent Order of the State of Texas (SPJST) that drew Clarence Sefcik in Granger (top).

Begun in 1862 in Prague during the height of Austrian rule, the Sokol is both an athletic and a political organization. Founder Dr. Miroslav Tyrš intended for the organization to affirm classical ideals of healthy mind and body through gymnastics training while instilling its members with a Czech national consciousness. Later, both the Nazis and the communists suppressed the Sokol, though it flourished in other countries around the world.

Texas once had twenty Sokol chapters, but participation declined dramatically after World War II. Seven chapters operate today, at Dallas, Fort Worth, West, Ennis, Houston, Corpus Christi and, most recently, Taylor. Faced with an assimilation process that has accelerated in the post-war years, the Sokol, like other Texas-Czech organizations, is seeking to expand its membership beyond the Texas-Czech community. Gymnastics training is the principal emphasis of the Texas Sokol, while instruction in Czech history (part of the original nineteenth-century Sokol program) is absent.

Sokol members perform at the Texas State Fair in Dallas (above and opposite page, above), while their Ennis counterparts march in the annual parade to kick off the Ennis Polka Festival (opposite page, below).

Five minutes to curtain, and suddenly screaming, teasing children fall silent. Excitable faces now look sullen, even fearful. Some sit huddled in corners, hunched over scripts, while others peak nervously through cracks in the backdrop at the first performances. Opposite page, fourth grader Krysta Janak awaits her turn to go on stage. Parents and relatives of students at the Vysehrad School have

come from across Lavaca County for the Christmas plays that high-light the year at the little school of eighty-two students.

"'Small school for a strong foundation,' that's our motto," says Vysehrad superintendent James Hermes, who teaches history and math and occasionally substitutes as bus driver. The Vysehrad School District, established in 1887 by local Czechs, was typical of the one-room country school system that provided elementary education across rural Texas and survived the public school consolidation process of the 1940s. The Czechs arrived with a strong appreciation for education, and often a settlement's first communal act was to pool meager resources to build a school.

Superintendent Hermes takes great pride in the amount of family involvement at Vysehrad, whether it be for Thanksgiving dinner (opposite page, above) or choosing a new staff member. "A lot of the old-world values are still here," he says, "and parents really want to be a part of their children's education." Sports occupy a secondary role at Vysehrad, with no after-school practices. "Those kids have chores to do when they get home," says Hermes.

Family Portrait
The Knapeks of Granger and Taylor

As the vast majority of Czech settlers in Texas once did, George, Johnny (opposite page, above, right), and Joe (opposite page, above, left) Knapek farm cotton and raise milo, wheat, maize, and cattle. Beginning around the middle of August, they harvest by stripping the cotton and dumping it into a module builder, an enormous machine that compresses the cotton into giant bricks (like the one George is covering with a tarp, opposite page, below) that will be picked up by the local ginning company. Cotton harvests vary greatly from year to year, even field to field, depending on climatic conditions and pests that can ruin one field but leave the next unharmed. With crop prices stagnant and the costs of pesticide and fertilizer climbing ever higher, the three brothers barely break even from the twelve-hundred acres they toil. "I guess it's a lot like gambling," says George, showing me a cotton plant ruined by weevils. "And sometimes it gets so dry, you just have to hope the good Lord sends you some rain."

Though their children participate in the labor of the farm (above, Bernard, Cynthia, and Jenny, George's and Joe's children, get ready to pull weeds from the cotton fields), most plan on a university education and careers other than farming.

"We was in the cotton field, the sun wasn't up yet. We'd pick till dark every day," says the brothers' mother, Mary, shown above surrounded by grandchildren and great-grandchildren on her eighty-sixth birthday. Born in Senice na Hané, Moravia, Mrs. Knapek came to Texas at the age of two, settling with her parents near Granger. She speaks mainly Czech with her children ("I didn't even learn to talk English until World War II," she says), who speak a mixture of Czech and English with one another, often switching between the two languages in mid-sentence. Johnny's son Anthony, thirty-three, is among the youngest in the family to still speak the language fluently.

Like most Texas Czechs, the Knapeks are Catholic, and some of the more traditional aspects of Texas-Czech culture remain strong among them. Johnny plays guitar in the Fritz Hodde and the Fabulous Six polka band (opposite page, above), and his wife Toni crochets delicate lace that she donates to local churches (opposite page, below).

Cotton was once king in most parts of Czech-settled Texas, though since the early 1960s there has been a sharp decline in its profitability. New industries have emerged to replace the crop: farmers have turned to cattle in Lavaca County (above, with Saints Cyril and Methodius Church of Shiner visible in the background) and small manufacturing operations have become an important alternative. In Shiner, Cathy Caka (opposite page, above) found full-time employment at Kaspar Wire Works, which since World War II has emerged as Shiner's biggest employer. More recently, new drilling methods have created a boom in the oil exploration industry (opposite page, below). "People in this area have a tremendous work ethic," says Josh Kaspar, advertising manager at Kaspar Wire Works, whose company has become the largest manufacturer of coin-operated newspaper vending machines in the nation.

The Flatonia Little League team had a less-than-stellar season, though that did not diminish the enthusiasm of their coach, thirty-six-year-old Tim Masek. Masek, unlike most Texas Czechs of his generation in Fayette and Lavaca counties, chose to resist the urban pull that has left both counties with average population ages of over sixty. Though he lived in Houston during his training as an electrician, he came back to start his own business and bring up his family. "I couldn't appreciate living here until I'd moved away," he explains, citing Flatonia's lack of crime, traffic, and pollution and the familiarity of his community. "You pick your own pace of life out here. If we want to go into Austin, we can just get in the car and go—it's not that far," he says.

Tim's sister Peggy Mica, however, did move away—to a life in Austin working as a computer science teacher. "I didn't expect it to be tough, but it was," she says of her departure seven years ago, remembering the closeness of her family and their involvement with the church at Praha. Being married to a fellow Texas Czech from Flatonia has helped, she says, as does her involvement with the Catholic Church in Austin. Though Mica does not speak Czech, she intends to pass on the values she has grown up with to her recent newborn, including a strong sense of family, trying hard to do one's very best, and pride in her ethnic heritage. "I sing the baby some of the Czech songs I remember, and when she sneezes I tell her 'bless you' in Czech. I try to teach her what I can," she says.

Family Portrait
The Klams of Dubina

For Ronnie Klam and his uncle Emil (above), thorough cleanup after a day of sausage making is as important as the preparations before. Just as they haven't wasted any of the hog they butchered, they don't waste water in washing their utensils. Such actions are typical of *hospodářství*, a concept central in the traditional Texas-Czech value system that places great emphasis on careful attention to detail and the frugal use of resources.

Hospodářství enables Ronnie and his wife Debbie to support themselves and their three sons from the modest income they earn from his jobs as a baker and frycook and hers as a bookkeeper and Amway representative. Though Ronnie and Emil both speak Czech, the rest of the family does not, and though Ronnie and Debbie admit that some of the more traditional aspects of Texas-Czech life will likely not survive in their children, they feel their value system will. "They might not carry on some of the traditions or speak the language, but

they'll still work hard and have that sense of responsibility," says Debbie.

A birthday party for several of the Dubina children, including the Klams' youngest son Josh (above), illustrates the closeness of the Dubina community that has given the Klams a further reason to stay. "It's a real good place to bring up a family," says Debbie.

For the many Texas Czechs who have moved to the big cities, the anonymity and impersonality that contrasts so sharply with the rural, ethnic context of their youth provides incentive to reestablish a sense of connection to their ethnic identity. Some organize into ethnic heritage groups, like the Austin Czech Historical Society, shown opposite page, below, inducting a new member. Other urban Texas-Czech societies, like the Catholic Czech Club of Dallas (above), have become social organizations that sponsor dances, ethnic celebrations, singing groups, and other activities for their members. The various Texas-Czech fraternal organizations also play a strong role in maintaining the ethnic solidarity of urban Texas Czechs, especially the SPJST with its prominent lodge in Dallas that often hosts Kovanda's Czech Band (opposite page, above).

Kovanda's is one of the few remaining Czech-style brass bands (in Czech known as *dechovka*) in Texas. "We don't ad-lib," says clarinetist Steve Kutra (in center of picture), "we play it like it's written." Vlastimil Kovanda, a Czech émigré who has since returned to the Czech Republic, started the band ten years ago and still sends the band music from Prague. Going to the church picnics at Frydek in

Austin County when he was young, Kutra remembers the brass orchestras that would play with their full compliment of instruments.
Asked what has highlighted his time with the band, Kutra recalls
one fan in particular: "During a break she came up and said: 'This
music, this must be Heaven!'"

"I dance the beseda because I'm Czech," explains Kelli Kopecky, fifteen, who performs the traditional dance several times a year with her beseda group at SPJST Lodge #84 in Dallas. The dance is meant to represent Bohemian, Moravian, Silesian, and Slovak cultural survival under Austro-Hungarian oppression. Multiple circles of four couples perform the complex combination of four separate dances, each one meant to represent a different region. "My responsibility is to pass on the pride," said Justine Yeager, president of Lodge #84, who has worked hard to get the younger generations involved in activities at the lodge and likes the feeling of attachment in being a part of Dallas's Texas-Czech community. Though she claims Lodge #84 can still come up with ten beseda circles (totaling eighty dancers), she admits some performers take a little prodding. "There's nothing like good old-fashioned guilt," she says.

Unlike their urban counterparts, the Czech Folk Dancers of West don't mind altering original Czech, Moravian, and Slovak dances in order to appeal to the tastes of their audience. "The beseda is a beautiful dance, but if people don't understand it they think it's boring," says Maggie Grmela, leader of the group, which performs annually at Westfest (above) and at folklife and ethnic events throughout the year (once even in the former Czechoslovakia). Some of the approximately twenty dancers have joined in the footsteps of parents or siblings. "I think they do it for the camaraderie and the fun most of all, and out of a sense of some small thing to preserve tradition," explains dancer Terry Sefcik, who has been with the group since its inception in 1976. Group members work together to choreograph new dances that often reflect Texan and Czech heritage.

More typical of Texas-Czech music is the style referred to as polkabilly—Czech polka and waltz music adapted to modern instrumentation with a structure that is shortened and simplified. Polkabilly has widespread appeal across the state, which culminates in the annual awards given by the Texas Polka Music Association. At the 1994 awards in Sealy, the Vrazels Polka Band from Buckholts (opposite page) walked away with the Polka Band of the Year award. Approximately seventy polkabilly bands play throughout Texas, some booked at events years in advance.

Among the more popular polkabilly bands are the Donnie Wavra

Orchestra, the Bobby Jones Czech Band, the Lee Roy Matocha Orchestra, the Leroy Rybak Orchestra, the Dujka Brothers, the Jodie Mikula Orchestra, and the Leo Majek Orchestra. "I know the people, it's one big family," says Bobby Jones of his fans. Jones is not of Czech descent but became inspired by the accordion playing of a high-school friend's father and has been a professional polka musician since age eighteen.

Radio stations throughout the state broadcast Texas-Czech music, among them KVLG out of La Grange. Lee Roy Matocha (opposite page, above) hosts the daily programs out of his Fayetteville studio, and is the last disc jockey in Texas to still do his show partially in Czech. Matocha maintains a close rapport with his listeners, taking requests and announcing birthdays. "That puts 'em on cloud nine, except when they're already dead," he says.

Whether at the Texas Polka Music awards or a dance contest at the Hallettsville Sausage Fest (opposite page, below), Texas-Czech music draws a faithful following. Some songs, like "A já sám," "Louka zelená," and "U studánky" originate from the old country, while others, like "Krásná Amerika," were written in Texas. When I asked one fan what he thought of Elvis Presley's music in comparison with Czech music, he replied: "I wouldn't give a penny for his songs."

Though the instrument has fallen from popularity, the hammer dulcimer was once prominent in several early Texas-Czech bands. Common among folk orchestras in Central and Eastern Europe, several Texas-Czech craftsmen made hammer dulcimers in Texas, among them Ed Krenek, father of Ray Krenek (opposite page, above), probably the last Texas-Czech hammer dulcimer player in the state. Though he still plays the instrument solo at special events, Ray does not incorporate it into his present band, where he plays the saxophone and the fiddle. "If you don't play the country music nowadays you don't get hired," he says.

Unlike the dulcimer, the accordion certainly has not lost its vitality among Texas Czechs, including these women (opposite page, below) near Shiner in Lavaca County who get together informally to play the Czech songs they have known since their youth. The songs provide a very emotional link to a past whose original Czech-Moravian culture is greatly diminished today; for Innoc Tofel of Ammannsville (above), whose father was a local musician, a song like "Sirotek" ("The Orphan") is a sad and beautiful reminder of the culture he knew as a child.

One scholar has noted that "next to the Czech language, music has always been the single most cohesive force in Texas-Czech culture," a statement that still holds true today. Though polka shows mainly draw the older generations, the music's attraction is not lost on the young. Some of these young listeners are drawn to it out of an appreciation for their ethnic heritage, while for others it's something they've been accustomed to since early childhood and participate in as a matter of course.

Family ties have always played a strong role among Texas Czechs and have helped their culture to cross from one generation to the next. And though intrastate migration among Czechs in Texas is frequent, scattering families across the state, family networks remain strong, culminating in annual family reunions that serve as an important way to maintain contact. Approximately three hundred Martinka descendants showed up at this reunion in Corn Hill; some family reunions, like for the Janaks of Hallettsville and Shiner, draw several thousand.

Annette Janecka chose a Czech waltz, "U studánky," as the song she would dance to with her father on her wedding night. Though she grew up in Houston, she remembers coming to visit her grandparents at Weimar as a child on weekends and attending mass at Saint Michael's Church. "I wanted a real Czech wedding," she says, "with the full mass, lots of family, the grand march—I like all the tradition." Her father, Charles Janecka (dancing with his daughter in opposite page, below), moved away from the area near Weimar where he was born after returning as a veteran from World War II. "When I came back there was nothing there," he explains. "You either worked in a filling station or on a farm, and that was it. I liked it out there but I just couldn't stay."

On the Sunday before All-Souls Day, Agnus Rhode (above) spent much of the day arranging flowers at the grave of her parents and other family members in Fayetteville. Also known as *dušičky*, the event is an important part of Texas-Czech tradition, though its significance to Czech Texas is even greater. For with every elderly Texas Czech who dies, so dies an irreplaceable link in Texas-Czech culture. Whether at a cemetery in Fayetteville or a gravesite at Krasna (opposite page, above), only stones, names, and memories attest to the lives and experiences of Texas Czechs who created a modern culture so unique in America's melting pot.

Opposite page, below, a plaque attests to the nine young men from Praha killed in World War II. They are honored every November 7 when veterans from around Texas converge on the little community for memorial services in honor of their fallen comrades.

A combination of religious and ethnic celebration, the annual August 15 Pražská Pout' or Praha Feast is the most important of the many annual Texas-Czech fests, and attracts thousands of Texas Czechs from across the state. Among the visitors in 1993 was Bishop Vojtěch Cikrle of Brno, capital of Moravia, who led a Czech-language mass and afterward mingled with crowds eager to shake his hand (above). A procession marks the beginning of the celebration (opposite page, below) that, despite the summer heat, draws many Texas Czechs, both young and old, in ethnic dress.

JOURNEYS INTO CZECH-MORAVIAN TEXAS

Perhaps the most beautiful physical relic of Czech settlement in Texas are the many churches built by the early immigrants. Of these, probably the most spectacular is Saint Mary's at High Hill (above), built in 1906. Its style is a mixture of Romanesque and Gothic Revival, and its ornate, wood-carved altars are typical of nineteenth-century Central European altars. Saint Mary's at Praha (left) features an interior frieze that depicts churches at Velehrad and Olomouc in Moravia, and paintings or statues of Czech saints, including Saint Jan of Nepomuk, Saint Ludmila and Saints Cyril and Methodius (the last two are the patron saints of Moravia). And at Dubina, Texas bluebonnets bloom in front of Saints Cyril and Methodius Church (opposite), a structure typical of the wooden Texas-Czech Catholic churches also built at Holman and Hostyn that no longer exist. Other beautiful Texas-Czech churches include the ones at Ammannsville, Moravia, Shiner, Wallis, East Bernard, Corn Hill, Sweet Home, and Weimar, as well as the Brethren church at Wesley.

"I just wanted to inspire people to spend their money less on material things, and also to demonstrate the values of the Slavic people," says Kevin Hannan, who commissioned the construction of a little chapel or *kaplička* on his parents' farm just outside of Taylor (opposite page). He modeled the chapel after one he photographed in southern Moravia in the Czech Republic; the exterior painting by post-1948 Czech émigré Zdenka Matula (opposite page, below, at left) is typical of Central European folk art with its incorporation of religion and nature.

The churches play a prominent role in the lives of the Texas Czechs they serve, from birth until death. Above, a first communion takes place at Ascension of Our Lord Church in Moravia, Texas.

Though much simpler in design than its Catholic counterparts, the Brethren church at Wesley is beautiful in its own right. Built in 1866, it was the first Brethren church in Texas, and Father Bohuslav Emil Lacjak, its first pastor, painted its unique interior. Though the church has been superseded by a newer structure, it is still used occasionally for meetings. A 1980 *Historic Structures Report* by Freeman and Doty Associates describes the building: "The merging of Czech cultural and architectural traditions with the building technologies and styles that existed in mid-nineteenth-century Texas produced a building that is evocative of the origins and traditions of the Czechs who built it. At the Wesley Church there exists a sense of place and a timeless quality that is the stuff of great architecture. There exists a spirituality that only certain buildings possess."

Since 1914, the Brethren Church has sponsored the Jan Hus School Encampment, now located at New Tabor in Burleson County, to promote future leadership within the Brethren Church. The students in the five-week summer program learn to establish a personal connection to God, and also study the Bible, music, spiritual development, and the history of the Czech-Moravian Brethren. "Without

that facility we wouldn't have stayed a denomination," says Joyce Baletka, former codirector of the school, citing conflicts within the Brethren Church in the 1960s that greatly undermined its vitality. Below, students Christie Polasek (foreground) and Tricie Conners sing on the last evening's outdoor excursion.

Of all the Texas-Czech settlements, none has put its ethnic identity to better commercial use than West. Taking advantage of its location on the state highway that connects Dallas and Austin, West advertises its Czech restaurants, gift shops, and bakeries with billboard signs to attract passing motorists. For Al and Patsy Picha (opposite page, above), business has been so good that they recently opened a second Czech-American Restaurant at West's cattle auction center.

Though the Pichas offer roast pork and "Czech-style" potatoes, they admit most customers prefer the standard menu. "If we didn't have chicken-fried steak we'd be up the creek," says Mrs. Picha.

Famous all over Texas, the town's annual Westfest has proven a great moneymaker. Begun in the 1970s by non-Czechs who had been inspired by the success of Texas-German festivals, the two-day September celebration draws up to forty thousand visitors, including students from nearby Baylor University (above). For the week before Westfest, the town is adorned with Czech flags (opposite page).

Jan Vaculik is editor and owner of *Hospodář,* Texas' other Czech-language newspaper. Originally printed in Omaha, Nebraska, the paper was bought by the Čechoslovák Publishing Co. of West in 1961 and consolidated with *Čechoslovák,* another West Czech-language publication. During the communist years, *Hospodář* was the only American newspaper allowed into Czechoslovakia, and today six hundred issues of its fourteen hundred circulation still go to the Czech and Slovak Republics every month. Like *Našinec, Hospodář* is written largely by its readers, who contribute whatever they feel like writing about, though its content is often more intellectual than that of *Našinec.* "It's like the roulette," explains Vaculik, a post-1968 Czech émigré who bought the paper in 1989. "You've got a bit of everything, everything you can dream of will eventually be in *Hospodář.*"

Anna Pelucha came to Lavaca County on her own at the age of sixteen from the little village of Rychaltice in Moravia. Though she has lived in Texas ever since, in seventy-four years she has never learned English beyond a few words and phrases. "She just never needed it growing up," explains her granddaughter Rene Meyer. "There were Czech newspapers and radio stations, and the people in the stores she'd go to, they all spoke Czech too." Communication between grandmother and granddaughter is a rather unique process, for Ms. Meyer knows practically no Czech. "We usually figure out what the other one is trying to say, and sometimes I can get one of the other ladies to help translate," says Ms. Meyer of her weekly visits to the nursing home. "What we talk about isn't so important anyway. It's more important that I'm just there."

"It's lonesome now, it's sad," says Bessie Striz, eighty-five, who has lived in the former coal mining area of Lyra in southern Palo Pinto County all her life. Her parents, immigrants from southern Moravia, settled at Lyra at the turn of the century, and both her father and her husband died due to ailments contracted working in the mines. "They worked hard. Nothing was given to them," she says. Today, she is the last fluent Czech speaker in the area; the SPJST hall at Lyra is gone, and Czech families, with names like Mesicek, Kriksajs, Hlavsa, and Mensik, have moved away.

When Danny Urbanovsky was his grandson Kevin's age, he remembers that being Czech made life difficult growing up in the little town of West. "When I was a kid I was never proud of being Czech," he says. "A lot of the Czechs were poor and didn't speak much English. I remember kids at school used to call us 'Bohunk,' and I was ashamed." The term "Bohunk" is a derogatory form of "Bohemian," the latter being the more common word non-Czechs used for the Czech immigrants well into the 1930s. Though most Texas Czechs have their roots in Moravia, many describe themselves in English as "Bohemian," even when they may use the term *Moravci* when speaking Czech. Many Texas Czechs I met were unclear about the distinction between "Czech," "Bohemian," and "Moravian."

Tommy Rainosek is the archetypal *hospodář*. A carpenter by profession, Rainosek, forty, is also skilled as a blacksmith and believes in doing what he can himself, whether it be conserving his own pickles and mushrooms or building his own drill rig. He credits his abilities to his father: "Now he could build just about *anything*," he says. Rainosek has grown up in the little settlement of Dubina in Fayette County, where he spoke only Czech until the age of five. Today, Rainosek is an officer of the KJT, the Czech Catholic Union of Texas, one of the several Texas-Czech fraternals that provide life insurance. Though his children do not speak Czech, he hopes to pass on the honesty, the inventiveness, and the work ethic that he feels stem from his Texas-Czech roots and have shaped his character.

Rainosek remembers that relations were once less than cordial between the local Czechs and Germans. "You just didn't go into the other's area alone," he remembers his father telling him. Many immigrants harbored old-country animosities, and Rainosek remembers how angry his father became when Rainosek's older brother announced his plans to marry a German.

Though Mark Halata, twenty-seven, grew up in the Houston suburb of Pasadena, he thinks the weekends he spent at Moravia visiting his family and hanging out at the Moravia Store listening to local musicians had a greater effect on who he is today. Musicians like Wence Shimek, the Vrazels, and the Joe Patek Band inspired his love for Texas-Czech polka and waltz music and convinced him to learn to play the accordion at an early age. "When I used to listen to tapes at home other kids would be like 'What the hell is that?'" he says. When Halata has time away from his job as an air-conditioning unit installer he plays in a band that blends different regional styles, and in 1993, he played at the Czech Fest in Rosenberg.

Fred Vinklarek, seventy-seven, is the last Texas Czech in the little community of Steen on the line between DeWitt and Gonzales counties. "I'm the only one left. All the others are dead, their kids all moved away—Houston, San Anton', Austin," he explains. Eight to ten Czech families once lived at Steen, farming cotton and corn and sending their children to Steen's little school. "I have some nephews over at Hochheim, but they ain't Czech—they don't speak the language," he says.

"We had it rough then," says Annie Martinek, eighty-seven, of her and her husband, Joe, who farmed cotton on their farm at the little settlement of Crisp just north of Ennis. Like many of the Czech settlers, they struggled to make a living from the land and to raise their family. "I had to take my babies in the field when we was farmin' cotton. Joe made me a little box that fit on the plow for me to put my youngest," she says. Unlike most of the Czechs who came to Texas, the Martineks' parents came from Bohemia rather than Moravia. Yet the Czech they speak with one another today incorporates elements of Moravian dialects, evidence of the strong Moravian influence over Texas-Czech culture.

For fifteen-year-old Erin Janak (right), being Czech has meant a strong connection to the Catholic church at Praha and having a grandmother who still milks her own cows and bakes kolaches from scratch. "I always think of Czech as the Church, . . . it's tradition for me," she says. A member of the KJZT Youth Group, she has sacrificed her Saturday mornings to learn to dance the beseda and make pastries, as well as to do charity work and religious study. Though she plans to go to college and eventually move to Austin, Erin wants to hold on to the qualities that make Czech people different. "Material things aren't so important to them, and their lives aren't so rushed," she says.

Little Trey Ging, grandson of Joe Knapek (see the preceding Knapek family portrait) is growing up in an environment still thick with Texas-Czech culture. His grandparents and several of his uncles speak Czech fluently and have preserved their Texas-Czech way of life, and Texas-Czech tradition at nearby Granger still runs strongly. Yet the number of Czech speakers in the state is diminishing rapidly, as is traditional Texas-Czech culture. Trey will likely never learn to speak more than a few words of Czech, and though the culture may re-main evident in the values that guide him in later life, one can only wonder if he will retain his sense of connection to a Texas-Czech ethnic and personal identity. For ultimately it is that personal identification, more than tradition, language, or any other cultural factor, that will mark the survival of Czech Texas.

Notes

1. Špaček Family. *Památník Rodiny Špačkové a Jejich Spříbuzněných Rodin,* p. 12.
2. Machann and Mendl, *Krasna Amerika,* p. 144.

Part 3

Czech-Moravian
Texas Today

Kde domov můj, kde domov můj?
Kde se rodí kukuřice
A bavelna ještě více
Kde ten sladký melas je a špeku nechybuje
A to je ta krásná země, zem Texaská, domov můj,
　　zem Texaská, domov můj.
Kde domov můj, kde domov můj?
Školy máme vystaveny, aji špolky založeny
Moravské i anglické, sláva nám vždycky rostě
A to je ta krásná země, zem Texaská, domov můj,
　　zem Texaská, domov můj.[1]

(Where is my home, where is my home?
Where corn sprouts
And cotton even more
Where there's sweet molasses and bacon isn't lacking
It's that beautiful country, the land of Texas which is my home,
The land of Texas which is my home.

Where is my home, where is my home?
We've built our schools and founded our fraternals
Our Moravian and English glory will ever grow
It's that beautiful country, the land of Texas which is my home,
The land of Texas which is my home.)

　　　　　　　　"Kde Domov Můj?" (Texas version)
　　　　　　　　—from Rose and August Konvicka
　　　　　　　　Moravia, Texas, 1994

Population

"How many Texas Czechs are there today?" has been one of the most difficult questions to answer in this project. In the process of my research, I have heard five-hundred thousand, eight-hundred thousand, even a million, though there are several reasons to doubt the accuracy of any of these figures. The first is that several scholars make no reference to the source of their estimate at all, while others seem to base their estimates on the figures of 350,000 to 500,000 "given for the total Czech population in Texas" in 1932 by Henry Maresh and Estelle Hudson.[2] The two authors appear to cite the U.S. Bureau of Immigration's *Annual Report by the Commissioner General to the Secretary of Labor of 1932,*[3] though a thorough examination of this document reveals no estimate whatsoever of the number of Czechs living in Texas. Also, these numbers do not coincide with the census figures of that period. As mentioned in Part 1, the census of 1940 gives a total of 62,680 Texans whose first language was Czech. Because some Texas Czechs were already growing up without any kind of Czech-language instruction by the 1940s,[4] the actual number of Texans of Czech descent was likely higher, though certainly not by almost 290,000! Also, according to Terry Jordan of the Department of Geography at the University of Texas at Austin, no overall records

of per-state ethnic composition were kept by the federal government until the census of 1980 (as opposed to the 1940 census's first-language categorization).[5] Hudson and Maresh's book, though it is a valuable contribution to the histories of specific immigrant families, lacks real credibility because of the absence of a bibliography.

Also, Jordan points out the natural, though perhaps unintentional, tendency of any ethnic group to exaggerate the size of its population. No doubt the same has happened with population estimates given by Texas-Czech scholars and organizations.

Certainly the most reliable source of population statistics is the 1990 census, though it too produces some questionable estimates. It states that there are 191,754 Texans who claim full, first, or second (partial) Czech ancestry. Of these, 90,808 claim Czech as their only ancestry,[6] giving Texas the highest Czech population of any state in the country.[7] However, several reasons make it likely that the real number of Texans who are of full or partial Czech descent is substantially higher. First, approximately 16 percent of respondents did not report their ancestry at all or simply listed themselves as "American."[8] Though most Texas Czechs I encountered seemed proud of their ethnicity, considering the nature of how I worked, I probably never met those who have no interest in their ethnicity. And it should not be assumed that this latter group is numerically insignificant. There were Czechs who arrived in Texas fully prepared to embrace their new homeland by dropping their original ethnic identity.[9] And many Texas Czechs in the post-World War II era moved to the big cities, where their rate of assimilation and loss of ethnic identity was much higher than in the rural areas.

Even if the same percentage of those who did not respond or listed themselves simply as "American" are actually of Czech descent, as for the Texas population as a whole, the census figure for the Texas-Czech total would only increase by about thirty thousand. However, a much larger potential pool of Czech descendants lies in the census section relating to second ancestry, since 77 percent of those surveyed never responded or could not be classified.[10] Reexamining the figures above, it is surprising that the number of Texans claiming full Czech ancestry (90,808) is so close to the number claiming partial Czech ancestry (100,946). Though Czechs in Texas traditionally preferred their children to marry other Czechs, by the 1940s, intermarriage with other ethnic groups seems to have been common and largely accepted. Especially in the post-war generations, married couples who are both full or part Czech are certainly the exception rather than the rule.[11] How many of those 13,103,020 people whose second ancestry is unknown or whose response was unclassifiable are of partial Czech descent is anyone's guess. Yet if the proportion is the same as for those Texans who did respond, then there are an additional 339,077 Texans of partial Czech descent.[12] It is very unlikely that the actual number is this high, though it does suggest that there are more Texas Czechs than accounted for by the 1990 census.

There is a third reason to dispute the census number for Texas Czechs, which is suggested by the membership totals of the Texas-Czech fraternal and mutual aid organizations. Together the RVOS, the SPJST, the *Česká Římsko-Katolická Podpůrná Jednota Žen Texaských* (KJZT), and the KJT have approximately 170,000 individual members,[13] of which the organizations estimate approximately 75 percent, or 127,500, are of Czech descent.[14] When compared to the census total, this would mean that about 67 percent of all Texas Czechs have claims with one of the four insurance companies. Though no data exist by which to judge such a figure, based on my own experience that number appears too high, especially among urban Texas Czechs. Though allegiance to the fraternals is still strong, such a high membership rate seems out of proportion with the general decline of Czech-Moravian culture and identity in Texas.

One other note on the 1990 census: if one compares the number of Texans claiming Czech descent to the numbers claiming Polish or Slovak descent, the result may seem strange. The latter two show much higher rates of response in relation to their rates of original immigration to Texas.[15] This anomaly is likely explained by the post-World War II demographic changes within the United States that brought Americans of Polish and Slovak decent to Texas. This hypothesis is supported by the 1990 census figures for Texans claiming use of Slovak or Polish language at home, both of which are much lower than equivalent statistics for Texas Czechs.[16]

So how many Texas Czechs are there? With the empirical evidence we have, that question is difficult to answer. But considering the preceding discussion, the 191,754 given by the 1990 census is easy to debate and an estimate of 300,000 to 400,000 does not seem unreasonable. Though one can dispute the significance of Czech ancestry in people who do not even bother to mention it on a questionnaire, an accurate total population count is essential to gaining proper insight into the vitality of continued Texas-Czech culture and ethnic identity. For in any examination of Czech-Moravian Texas, those Texas Czechs who feel no connection to their ethnic heritage are just as significant as those who have maintained their ethnic identity.

Ethnic Identity

Among Texas Czechs who are aware of their heritage, the perception of ethnic identity is not uniform and can even sound contradictory to an outsider. Its complexity is based on a mixture of archaic old country regional identities, misunderstandings of historical and modern-day geographic and national realities, problems in translating terms from Czech into English, an occasional lack of personal awareness of ethno-ancestral origins, and a reinterpretation of ethnic identity over successive generations.

In his 1985 study of Czech-Moravian culture in Texas, Kevin Hannan discusses the historically significant presence of an exclusively Moravian identity in Texas. The vast majority of immigrants from the Czech lands came to Texas before the creation of the Czechoslovak state, in a time when the future alliances of the different Slavic peoples had not been fully established and the present national identities of Central and Eastern Europe had not been clearly defined. Kevin Hannan states: "One important characteristic of the Czech-Moravian's culture has been his perception of national identity. This perception to a significant degree evolved from the concept of national identity which was prevalent in 19th century north-eastern Moravia. This concept, in which a distinctive Slavic and Moravian identity was stressed, does not correspond to the national identity held by the modern-day Czechoslovaks or even modern-day Moravians."[17]

The effect of this concept in Texas was that many early Czech-Moravian settlers had little or no perception of themselves as Czech, referring to themselves as "Moravci," a term used to describe Moravians who considered themselves ethnically, culturally, and linguistically distinct from Bohemian Czechs.[18] The currency of the term in Texas is evidenced by the observations of journalist Ludvík Dongres[19] in 1924 and from passages in the Texas-Czech newspaper *Svoboda*.[20] In my own encounters I heard again and again accounts by Texas Czechs of how their grandparents had stubbornly referred to themselves as "Moravian," and that a label of "Bohemian" was considered an offense, though today Texas Czechs who refuse the classification of "Czech" are rare.[21] Over the years it seems the importance of a separate Moravian identity in Texas has faded, though it is not extinct. According to the 1990 census, among the 191,754 Texans claiming Czech ancestry, 1,209 referred to their first or second ancestry as "Moravian."[22] This comprises only 0.63 percent of the total, but that it surfaces at all in 1990 is significant, since a majority of Texas Czechs I met had only a vague or incomplete understanding of distinctions between "Czech," "Bohemian," and "Moravian."

The reason for misunderstanding these terms lies not merely in cultural and geographic ignorance, but also in how the terms are translated from Czech. In English "Bohemia" and "Moravia" refer to two different geographic regions, while "Czech" can describe the people who inhabit both. However, in Czech the word for "Bohemia" is "Čechy," while the adjective "Czech" is "český." There is no word in the Czech language to distinguish "Czech" and "Bohemian." One other note on misused terms: sometimes I heard Texas Czechs use the term "Slavic" to describe a nationality or a region ("He was from Slavic"), a term some also confused with "Slovak." Again, the explanation is probably more complex than simple ignorance. Hannan cites the perception of a duel Slavic-Moravian national identity among the traits particular to northeastern Moravia that found affirmation among Texas Czechs.[23] Though the people I spoke to were likely unaware of the historical context of such an identity, it had possibly played enough of a role in their upbringing to infuse their perceptions of old country realities.

The difficulty in translating "Čechy" and "český" is partially responsible for another aspect of Texas-Czech identity, and that is the tendency for many to describe themselves as "Bohemian" rather than "Czech" or "Moravian," even when their ancestors came from Moravia. Also, Kevin Hannan has found that the term "Czech" did not gain currency in America until after the creation of the Czechoslovak state in 1918. And many Texas Czechs continued to use the more archaic "Bohemian"[24] to describe themselves in English well into the 1970s and early 1980s, even though they referred to themselves as "Moravian" when speaking Czech. The most striking example of this "Bohemian" identity came when I stopped once in the little settlement of Olmos in Bee County. I approached two older men by a farmhouse who (from the way they spoke English) I guessed were Texas Czechs. I asked them if anyone in the area still spoke Czech, and to my surprise they looked at me quizzically. Then one said: "No, nobody here speaks *Czech*. But quite a few people speak Bohemian." Though Bohemian dialects of Czech exist, never have I heard any reference to one as a distinct language from Czech. Rather, the more likely explanation of the man's response is that in his relatively isolated community, the term "Czech" had simply never caught on and people still used "Bohemian" in a way common in pre-1918 America.

Why would Texas Czechs refer to themselves as "Bohemian" even when their ancestry was Moravian, especially when Americans, perhaps in a reference to the gypsy association with "bohemian," sometimes used the term in a pejorative sense? After all, many people I talked to had adolescent memories of other children taunting them with "Bohemian" and the much worse "Bohunk," which in the earlier years was particularly offensive to Texas Czech–Moravians proud of their identity as *Moravci*. Over the years, perhaps as a way of avoiding having to explain to ignorant outsiders the exact meaning of the different terms (something later generations might not fully have been clear on themselves) and because the term was so common among people of other ethnic groups, "Bohemian" became an ethnic label many simply appropriated for themselves.

The Olmos example above suggests a broken or absent connection to the Czech Republic in the minds of some Texas Czechs, something I observed more than once. I remember one gentleman in particular whom I asked about the origins of his ancestors. He told me they came from the settlement of Pisek near Fayetteville, and when I pressed him further as to their old country origins, he seemed not to understand. He knew one grandmother had come from Germany, but he seemed to honestly believe that the rest of his family had always originated from the Fayetteville area.[25] Yet for him his Czech heritage still played a very important role: he spoke Czech fluently and had played in different family Czech polka/waltz orchestras most of his life. The significance of his perception is not his ignorance, but the strength of the early Czech-Moravian community in Texas: so completely did it fill the lives and needs of its members that some were growing up unaware of their foreignness in a new land.

At the other extreme, some Texas Czechs who visit the modern Czech Republic return to Texas with a strengthened sense of their own Czech-Moravian identity to a degree they never had before. People who find out their ancestors came from Moravian Wallachia may return proud to sing "My jsme Valaši," even if they had never been conscious of a Wallachian identity in their youth. In fact, it seems that those Texas Czechs who are most assimilated into mainstream America come back from the Czech Republic most enthusiastic to proclaim their Czechness or their Moravian heritage according to a modern cultural context that might be very different from the one known to their ancestors.[26]

Texas Czechs have recognized the decline of their original culture, and some are attempting to preserve and even revive it. "We became too Americanized. Now people are trying to make up for it, to get it back," said one gentleman I talked to.[27] Evidence of this effort is the Czech Heritage Society of Texas, founded in 1982. With over one thousand members and thirteen chapters, the organization has thus far sought primarily to assist Texas Czechs pursuing genealogical research, for which it established archives at the Jalufka House in Corpus Christi. However, its avowed purpose is "to preserve and promote the heritage, culture, genealogy and language of Czech Texas."[28] New president Caroline Meiners has promised to devote more attention to this mission.

Culture

In 1994, little is left in Texas of the original Czech-Moravian culture as known by the first-generation settlers. Rather, it is *Texas* Czech–Moravian culture that is still strong and finds expression through music, food, folk traditions, and crafts. One contributor to the demise of the original culture has been the absence of language instruction within the household for most of the post-war generations. Czech-Moravian culture in Texas was once rich in fairy tales, legends, proverbs, and children's games, all of which are elements of a folklore that simply does not translate effectively into English and requires the participation of children if it is to survive.[29] Other traditions that have specific material requirements not commonly available, such as the traditional Czech Christmas dinner of carp,[30] have decreased in popularity as well.

Texas Czech–Moravian culture has roots in the original cultural equivalents, with modifications originating from several factors: the tastes of an audience unfamiliar and hence not always responsive to the original culture; the blending of Texas and Czech-Moravian cultural elements that reflects a single rather than a dual ethnic and cultural identity; and efforts by more assimilated Texas Czechs to reaffirm the original culture in a way that reflects modern Czech, rather than original Czech-Moravian, culture. Each modifier affects Texas Czech–Moravian culture to varying degrees within the different forms of cultural expression.

MUSIC AND DANCE

The most evident expression of Texas Czech–Moravian culture is music, which reflects not only the three factors of change listed above, but also lingering traits of the original cultural forms as well. Throughout the year, Texas-Czech polka/waltz bands play at venues throughout the state. Some play only occasionally and locally, while others are booked years in advance from Fort Worth to Corpus Christi. The seventy to eighty bands find organized support among the Texas Polka Music Association and its monthly newspaper, *The Texas Polka News,* and the P. O. L. K. of A. (the Polka Lovers Klub of America), whose Texas chapter, with over one thousand members, is the largest in the nation. Most importantly, the music operates as a vital bridge between generations, drawing younger people into a culture that they may otherwise never experience.

As mentioned in Part 1, music has traditionally played an intrinsic role in the cultural life of Texas' Czech-Moravian settlements. Of the early orchestras, perhaps none was more famous than "Baca's Family Band," started by Frank Baca at Bordovice near Fayetteville in 1892. The band played at Czech and German settlements throughout Central Texas and was succeeded by later generations of Baca bands, including "Baca's Original Band and Orchestra," "Baca's New Deal Orchestra," and the "L.B. Baca Orchestra," all founded by children of Frank Baca. The bands developed their own styles, releasing records and incorporating swing and big band influences in the 1930s and 1940s.[31] Though the early

Baca bands played brass music typical of late nineteenth-century Bohemia, photographs of the first Baca band show use of the dulcimer,[32] an instrument typical of Moravian folk ensembles. Other musicians, like the Kreneks of Pisek and Ed Dybala of Ganado, also included the dulcimer in their instrumentation and even built their own,[33] though today the instrument is almost never played in Texas. Authentic Moravian folk music, characterized by its string instrumentation and unconventional meter, is entirely absent from the modern Texas-Czech musical tradition.

Texas-Czech polka/waltz bands today basically fit into two categories: *dechovka* (brass), characterized by strict musical interpretation and full range of instrumentation, and what one person has dubbed "polkabilly,"[34] characterized by simplified music and individual interpretation of original Czech songs coupled with modern instrumentation. Of the two, polkabilly is by far the more popular, and is also a more authentic expression of Texas-Czech culture. Bands with names like The Vrazels Polka Band, the Bobby Jones Czech Band, the Donnie Wavra Orchestra, the Leo Majek Orchestra, the Dujka Brothers, and the Jodie Mikula Orchestra play at polka fests, picnics, weddings, anniversaries, and other celebrations across Texas throughout the year and command a strong following. Most of the bands are comprised of five to eight musicians and typically include an accordion, a small brass section, an electric guitar, an electric bass and/or tuba, drums, and several vocalists. Some, like the Leo Majek Orchestra, are family bands that have kept their membership in the family over generations,[35] while others are relatively new and might have non-Czech members. Their songs are a mixture of original Czech, Texas-Czech, and Country and Western, though even the original Czech songs have been modified to accommodate modern instrumentation and a quicker tempo. Most of the polka and waltz songs are still sung in Czech, though many have their English-language equivalents, such as the Texas-Czech "Krásná Amerika," also known and sung as "Beautiful America."

Dechovka in Texas is much less common. I found only two Czech bands, the Dallas Czech Concert Orchestra and Kovanda's Czech Band, that fall into this category. These bands have consciously resisted the influences of Country and Western and other musical genres, attempting instead to preserve the authenticity of their music. "Kovanda's plays it as it was written," said Leland Miller,[36] general manager of the band, and his dedication to maintaining the original sound is typical of *dechovka* style. Instrumentation in Kovanda's includes two flügelhorns, two clarinets, two trumpets, baritone horn, euphonium, tuba, drums, and one vocalist. Most of their music is original, written by Vlastimil Kovanda, a post-1968 Czech émigré who founded the band in Houston and who has since returned to the Czech Republic.

Both Texas-Czech and *dechovka* polka/waltz music originate in the music of František Kmoch and Jaromil Vejvoda, who wrote songs, like the "Beer Barrel Polka," that became immensely popular, particularly in Bohemia, at the turn of the century. Many of the polkas and waltzes from this tradition, like "A já sám," "Louka zelená," and "Nemelem, nemelem" remain popular in Texas today. Personal interviews with older Texas Czechs suggest that *dechovka* was once much more common in Texas, though the style changed in response to economy and the desires of its audience. Though few Texas-Czech bands are fully professional, they nevertheless must fill dance halls if they hope to be rehired. "You gotta play what the audience wants to hear . . . If they're dancin', they're satisfied, but if they're sittin' down, you gotta play somethin' to get 'em up," said Lee Roy Matocha of the Lee Roy Matocha Orchestra.[37] He explained that no band can survive today by playing only polkas and waltzes. Most audience members I talked to favored the "peppier" sound of polkabilly, while those who preferred *dechovka* seemed drawn by the nostalgic, emotional effect of its old-world sound.

Though people over fifty were by far in the majority at most polka shows I observed, the music does seem to inspire significant enthusiasm among younger generations. Bands like Fritz Hodde and the Fabulous Six and the Leroy Rybak Orchestra include musicians in their mid-teens and early twenties, and the larger polka celebrations are well attended by people of all ages. Many young people I talked to perceived the music as something "Czech" and responded to it out of an apprecia-

tion of their own ethnic heritage, while for others it was something they had been accustomed to since early childhood and participated in as a matter of course.

The various polka/waltz orchestras are not the only source of Czech music in Texas; various choirs and singing groups across the state attract their own following by performing a mix of Czech-Moravian and Texas-Czech folk songs, religious hymns, polkas, and waltzes. Songs in the repertoire of the East Bernard Czech Singers include "Morava krásná zem" (Beautiful Moravia), "Hora Šinerská" (The Hills of Shiner), "Anděle boží, strážce můj" (My Guardian Angel) and "Červený šáteček" (Red Handkerchief Waltz).[38]

Because Texas-Czech music incorporates the vernacular language into a popular, ethnically based cultural experience—and because it commands a strong, emotional tie to many of its listeners[39]—it becomes an ideal vehicle for cultural continuity. Machann observes that "next to the Czech language, music has always been the single most cohesive force in Texas-Czech culture."[40] Change within the style and instrumentation of the music should not be viewed negatively, but rather as a natural evolutionary process whose roots remain undeniably within the original cultural context of the first-generation settlers. Machann notes, "it seems reasonable, then, to treat this process of musical change as one measure of cultural assimilation and, on the other hand, the persistence of traditional forms as a measure of resistance to assimilation."[41] Just as in biology, such evolutionary change is necessary if Texas-Czech music is to survive.

Various Texas-Czech dance groups perform as well, and they too can be placed in two distinct categories: those, like the Dallas Beseda Dancers of SPJST Lodge #84—who insist on a strict interpretation to ensure the authenticity of their performances—and others, like the Czech Folk Dancers of West, who have either adapted original Czech, Moravian, and Slovak folk dances to their own taste or choreographed new dances with the European ones as inspiration. The former is a more self-conscious effort at cultural preservation; their only dance, the beseda, is meant to represent Bohemian, Moravian, Silesian, and Slovak cultural survival under Austro-Hungarian oppression. Multiple circles of four couples perform the complex combination of four separate dances, each one meant to represent a different region. Since its founding in 1976, the latter group, on the other hand, has changed its repertoire in response to its audience. Leader Maggie Grmela said of the beseda, "It's a beautiful dance, but if people don't understand it, they think it's boring."[42] Not only have the West dancers modified the original forms, but they have also added musical and choreographic elements to reflect their Texas heritage, even down to the red handkerchiefs they wear around their necks in combination with their ornate Texas Czech–Moravian costumes.[43] Of the two styles, the latter is more popular; the West dancers perform throughout the year, and in 1988 even performed in Czechoslovakia.

The separate types of Texas-Czech music and dance groups reflect more than differing interpretations of cultural forms; they indicate a fundamental difference in urban and rural Texas-Czech ethnic identity. Assimilation and loss of original Czech culture and language among those who moved to the cities were higher than in rural communities, and those urban Texas Czechs who seek to recapture their ethnicity turn to what they see as more authentically Czech (hence, the lack of modification or improvisation among the Dallas Beseda Dancers or Kovanda's Czech Band of Houston). Whereas rural Texas Czechs, who seek to maintain the culture of their youth—a culture shaped by a hundred plus years of evolution in Texas—reflect a single Texas-Czech identity rather than a dual and dichotomized one. Though rural Texas Czechs may refer to themselves as "Czech" or "Moravian," they are in fact referring to what they know the terms to mean within a *Texas*-Czech context that includes its own, unique cultural forms.

KROJ

Nowhere is the existence of a single Texas-Czech identity more visually represented than in the *kroj*, or traditional folk costumes. In Bohemia and Moravia, these costumes represent regions and villages, and vary greatly in style, intricacy, and color. Women's costumes typically consist of black boots and stockings, a richly embroidered skirt trimmed with lace, pleated at the

waist and worn over several wool petticoats, a lace trimmed linen blouse with puffed shoulders under a tightly fitting dark-colored embroidered vest, and some kind of headdress to indicate marital status.[44] Men's costumes are simpler, with boots, embroidered, fitted pants, usually a white linen shirt, an embroidered vest, and occasional headdress. Some early Czech-Moravian settlers brought their *kroje* to Texas, and many of these original costumes have survived over generations. Other costumes have been recently imported by Texas Czechs visiting the Czech Republic.

In addition to the old-country *kroj,* many Texas Czechs have created their own costumes by incorporating original elements according to personal taste and available materials, and sometimes also by introducing Texas motifs. Bill Vornsand's costume on page 24 reflects a combination of Moravian folk elements with symbols, like bluebonnets and the map embroidered into his vest, to represent Texas. His black pants, black vest, and embroidered shirt are typical features of men's Texas-Czech costumes, which I've seen occasionally supplemented with a Texas-style bolo tie. Women's Texas-Czech costumes, such as Carol Mraz's on page 25, usually incorporate simpler lace and embroidery than their European counterparts and exclude the wool petticoats impractical in the Texas climate.

The costumes are most prominent at polka fests and other Czech oriented celebrations, and are also worn by Texas-Czech dance and singing groups. Their function as a visual representation of the statement "I'm Czech" is perhaps obvious, though the fact that some incorporate Texas motifs reflects the strength of a single Texas-Czech identity. Some Texas-Czech costumes I saw also incorporated personal elements, such as names of people or places,[45] showing not only that the costumes serve a similar purpose to the original ones from Bohemia and Moravia—namely as a form of localized expression often based on a strong sense of regional origin—but that the wearer likely has a strong emotional attachment to the costume and acknowledges its function as a form of individual, and not just ethnic, expression. Such a strong marriage of ethnic and individual identity speaks to the enduring nature of Texas Czech–Moravian culture.

FOOD

Texas-Czech food, like the other forms of Texas-Czech culture, has its roots in the traditions of the old country but has been adapted to its Texas context. Barbara Dybala describes her Texas-Czech cookbook, *Generation to Generation: Czech Foods, Customs, and Traditions, Texas Style* as "a project conceived to preserve another of the Czech arts, by giving you a taste of the past, but mixed with the next generations' modifications, and flavored with our rich Czech Traditions and History."[46]

The most typical Texas-Czech food is the *koláč*, a small, round pastry with a filling in the center that is most often poppy seed or cream cheese, though sometimes prune, apricot, cabbage or other fruit. Other Texas-Czech pastries include *klobásniky*, small pieces of sausage wrapped in dough, also called "pigs in a blanket"; *buchta*, a larger fruit-filled loaf; and strudel. Sausage too is an important part of the Texas-Czech kitchen. Some, like *jitrnice*, also called *jatrnice* (or head sausage), *jelita* (blood sausage), and *přezvuršt* (head cheese, in the modern Czech Republic referred to as *tlačenka*) are typical of sausage types found in the Czech Republic, while others, like the sausage made from pork and deer, are particular to Texas. Other important Texas-Czech staples include cabbage, potatoes, garlic, pickles, onions, and clabbered cheese.

Except for the *koláč* and the local family meat market typical of any Texas-Czech community, the food seems to have found little commercial application. The few Czech-American restaurants in Texas I found barely differ from the average Texas family restaurant, though the servings may be a little more generous. It seems such Texas classics as chicken-fried steak and barbecue are just as much a part of Texas-Czech cuisine as sausage and potatoes, while other elements of the Czech kitchen, such as the ubiquitous *knedlíky* (dumplings), are rare. At home the traditional recipes have been more strongly preserved, and only there can one find truly authentic Texas-Czech chicken noodle soup or potatoes with butter and onion. Most Texas-Czech families I met had maintained a strong sense of self-sufficiency, growing their own vegetables and often supplying their own chicken and pork. The *zabijačka*, or hog-butcher-ing, is a tradition most Texas Czechs I met remembered fondly at least from their childhood, if not from their present, experience.

CRAFTS

Most traditional Czech-Moravian crafts, like woodcarving, pottery, and egg-painting, have not survived in Texas, though the last may undergo a renaissance as Texas Czechs return from folk culture seminars in the Czech Republic. Though they are rare, I did find isolated examples of certain crafts, such as stained-glass making[47] and intricate lace work,[48] that are being continued. The only craft I found that is more widespread is quilt-making, which the Texas Czechs seem to have adopted from Anglo-American folk culture. I heard of quilt-making circles, including ones at Dubina, Moravia, and Bila Hora, where groups of elderly women would work together on a quilt and chat about local goings-on. Though I did not come across any such circles in my own fieldwork, I did meet several women who still make quilts, mostly to be sold at auction for the benefit of the local church. Styles in quilt design vary tremendously, and subject matter revolves around religion, nature, and community.

Language

Perhaps the most fascinating aspect of Texas-Czech culture is the continued use of the Czech language. Seventy-five years since the end of major Czech-Moravian immigration, it is still possible to hear Czech spoken in public (albeit rarely) around places like Praha, Granger, Ellinger, Fayetteville, Schulenburg, and La Grange. Estimates on the number of Czech speakers in Texas vary; one commonly referred to statistic by Texas Czechs is that their language is the third most spoken in Texas. Unfortunately, there is no evidence to support such a claim: the 1990 census reveals seven other languages in Texas beside English and Spanish spoken by more people at home than Czech.[49] However, Czech is the most widely spoken Slavic language, with 20,453 Texans claiming use of the language at home.[50] The actual number of Texans who can still speak or at least understand Czech is undoubtedly significantly higher, for many have either lost the habit of using it or no longer have other Czech speakers to communicate with. Even more significant is that some Texans still use Czech as their preferred language among family and close friends. And, incredible as it may seem, a handful of Texas Czechs have never gained a firm grasp of English, despite having lived nearly their entire lives in Texas.[51]

Decreasing Czech-language ability between generations is dramatic. In his 1991 study of Texas Czechs around the towns of Granger and Taylor, Woody Smith found people over the age of fifty to have a language retention "very much intact," though people tested in their thirties had for the most part "only a bare survival of the lexicon."[52] In my own observations I found that a majority of Texas Czechs over fifty, both in urban and rural areas, seem to understand and have at least a conversational speaking ability in Czech. Fluent Czech speakers in their forties were less common, and thirties or younger rare. Only in the most rural areas, like Ammannsville, Granger, and Ellinger, did I meet people thirty-five or younger who could speak Czech fluently. At twenty-seven, James Korenek (see page 27) was the youngest, though I heard about a little girl aged seven at Ammannsville who can still understand the language.

The language survives within a family most readily when both parents speak it with their children, and as more Texas Czechs intermarry with members of other ethnic groups, the Czech language's rate of survival to the next generation drops. However, I observed one very interesting phenomenon between ethnic Germans and Czechs who had intermarried. Again and again I noticed that the spouse who had originally grown up speaking German had not only learned Czech after marriage, and could often still speak Czech today, but had also lost the ability to speak German.[53] Gender did not seem to play a role, though the prevalence of Czech over German is perhaps explained by the effect of two world wars and the common use of Czech on social occasions.

Some ethnic Germans and Austrians came to Texas from German-speaking pockets in Bohemia and Moravia, and of these, some seem to have already had the ability to speak Czech before they arrived. One example is the settlement of Velehrad in Fayette County, where Ben Jurica, who owned the corner grocery store, told me nearly all the local Germans could speak Czech.[54] Occasionally members of other ethnic groups that worked and lived in Czech communities also learned to speak the language. I heard of African Americans at Granger, Fayetteville, La Grange, Cistern, Plum, and Abbott who spoke Czech fluently.[55] Unfortunately, none is still living.

Though speaking and comprehension ability in Czech are still strong in Texas, reading ability is not, which is hardly surprising considering the scarcity of Czech-language texts used today by people in their everyday lives. Though the Czech-language press in Texas once held a strong following, the present circulations of *Našinec* and *Hospodář* are small, and their readership seems based on habit and nostalgia rather than necessity. Aside from old books, newspapers, or magazines that have remained within the household, there is little other source in Texas for Czech-language texts.

However, even when the circulation of Czech-language newspapers reached their peak, the fact that most published in literary Czech did little to undermine one of the most interesting features of Texas-Czech and that is the survival of old country dialects.[56] Czechs who came to Texas spoke according to the dialectical areas of their origin, and because so many came from very concentrated areas in the Lachian and Wallachian regions of Moravia, the Czech spoken in Texas has many features of dialects specific to these regions. Even Czechs who did not come from northeastern Moravia acquired elements of these dialects in their speech, as did their children to an even higher degree.[57]

Kevin Hannan describes many of the phonological features common in Texas Czech, including shortened vowel sounds (where the standard Czech pronunciation of *ý, á, í,* and *é* is *y, a, i* and *e*), a characteristic specific to Lachian dialect; the palatalization of consonants *d, t,* and *n* when they follow an *i* or an *e,* as is common in both Lachian and Wallachian dialects; and placement of stress in a word on the penultimate syllable, as in Lachian and northern Wallachian dialects, as opposed to stress on the first syllable as in standard Czech.[58] In addition, I heard some Texas-Czech speakers soften the letter e, so that *postel* (bed) becomes *postěl* and *medvěd* (bear) becomes *mědvěd*. Also, many people pronounced certain words with an -*a* ending rather than the standard -*e*, so that *jalovice* (heifer) becomes *jalovica*, *vejce* (egg) becomes *vejca*, and *svině* (sow) becomes *sviňa*; and the Czech -*ou*, which has a very wide, open sound, in Texas Czech has a tighter -*u* sound. Both are features that Hannan identifies as archaic forms lost in modern, standard Czech and that characterize certain Moravian dialects.[59]

The influence of Moravian dialects on Texas Czech is not limited to phonology; lexicographical deviations from standard Czech exist as well. The following is a list of words and expressions I heard Texas Czechs use that are not found or are uncommon in modern, standard Czech.[60] The words fall into three categories: words that originate directly from one or several dialects, as well as German or Slovak; words that are common in standard Czech but in Texas Czech have other meaning(s), such as *maliny* and *prutko*; and words in Texas Czech that derive from English. When possible, I have indicated the origin of the word according to appropriate geographic regions of Moravia.[61] Note that these three areas are all in northeastern Moravia:

> *Wallachia, or Valašsko (V)—the approximate area between Bojkovice and Rožnov pod Radhoštěm; Lachia, or Lašsko (L)—between Frenštát pod Radhoštěm and Frýdek-Místek; and Teschen, or Těšínsko (T)—between Frýdek and Třinec.*

In addition, some words originate from Slovak (Sl) and German (G). When I could not find the specific Moravian geographic region of origin I have indicated simply "Moravian" (M).

Texas Czech	English	Standard Czech	Origin
jo	yes	ano	G
ja su	I am	já jsem	M
za malo	you're welcome	prosím, není zač	L
ogar	boy	hoch, chlapec	V
kluk	boy	hoch, chlapec	inter-dialectical

Texas Czech	English	Standard Czech	Origin
cerka	girl	děvče, dívka, holka	V, L
děvčatko	small girl	děvčatko	V, L, T
tož	well, so . . .	tak . . .	M, inter-dialectical
jejdanečky leute, leute . . .	oh my goodness approximate translation: "My, my . . ." or "Well, well . . ."	proboha, jé	archaic —from German, literally meaning "People, people . . ."
zumec	"no way" or "nothin' doin'" —probably from the standard Czech "vůbec," meaning "by no means"	-	?
špatny kram	"sorry thing"	-	L, T
pomaly a furt	slowly but surely	pomalu, ale jistě	
ešče	still, more	ještě	M
dneskaj	today	dneska, dnes	V
kaj	where to	kam	T, L
Kam deš?			V
Kaj jdeš?	(Stress on j in jděš.)		T, L
Kde jdeš?	(Stress on j in jděš.)		V
Kde deš?			V
	Where are you going?		
Kam jdeš?	(Stress on j.)		V
Z otkaj jsi?	Where are you from?	Odkud jsi?	L, T
Co viděš?	What do you see?	Co vidíš?	L, T
Ja čnu.	I read.	Já čtu.	?
tež	also	také	M (V, L)
lebo	or	nebo	Sl
anebo	or	nebo	inter-dialectical
špacyr	stroll	procházka	G
ščura	rat	krysa	T, L, V
stařenka	grandmother	babička	V
stařiček	grandfather	dědeček	V
poznot,	fingernail	dráp	M

Texas Czech	English	Standard Czech	Origin
paznecht	or claw		
dekl	lid	poklička	G
zabiját	to butcher	zabíjet	V, L, T
frafčak	train	vlak	?
krndal	knife	nůž	?
měch	sack	pytel	M
odlet	to urinate	močit	?
potem	then	potom, pak	V, L
klobasa	sausage	párek	L
	—see explanation below		
kotlačka, kobza	corn cob	kukuřičný klas	?
vartovat	to watch, look after	hlídat	G
háby	clothes	oblečení	M, Sl
prutko, prutčejs	quickly	rychle	?
špás	joke, fun	žert	G
špek	bacon	slanina	G
šlauf	hose, garden hose	hadice	G
blajvas	pencil	tužka	G
včil	now	ted'	M
besedovat	to visit	navštívit	
	—besedovat in standard Czech means to chat or to have a talk, though I heard it used in the sense of to visit, which in standard Czech is navštívit.		
picháče	thorn	trny, ostny	M
kobzole, kobzale (stress on penultimate syllable in both cases)			
	potatoes	brambory	L
zemjaky	potatoes	brambory	Sl
erteple	potatoes	brambory	G
brambory			Polish influence
	—stress on penultimate syllable, standard Czech takes stress on initial syllable		
kartofel	potato	brambory	G
paták	potato, sweet potato	brambor	?
patejk	sweet potato	sladký brambor	?
slunko	sun	slunce	inter-dialectical

Texas Czech	English	Standard Czech	Origin
kura	hen	slepice	Sl
kvočka	laying hen	kvočna	Sl
maliny	hackberries, mulberries, blueberries		?
	—standard Czech meaning is raspberries, while standard Czech for mulberries is moruše		
ogurek, ogurka	cucumber	okurka	Sl
krchov, kerchov	cemetery	hřbitov	G
kačena	duck	kachna	inter-dialectical
norka	turkey	krocan	M
jalufka, jalovica	heifer	jalovice	?, inter-dialectical
lože	bed	postel	archaic Czech
sesla	chair	židle, křeslo	G
polovjak	south	jih	?
obička	kidney	ledvina	?
šnuptichel	handkerchief	šátek, kapesník	G

Because of Austrian rule over Bohemia and Moravia, and because of the presence of German settlements in the Czech lands since the thirteenth and fourteenth centuries, German loan words in Moravian dialects are common. However, it is unlikely that these words in Texas Czech originate from the influence of Texas German.

Many Texas Czechs still understand and use the standard Czech equivalents, though not always. For instance, the Texas-Czech *jo*, meaning *yes*, is common in modern usage throughout the Czech Republic, though the standard Czech *ano* seems practically unheard of in many parts of Texas, as is the colloquial Czech greeting *ahoj*. Some words, such as *klobasa* and *prutko*, do not originate from a specific Moravian dialect, yet their usage in parts of Texas deviates from standard Czech. In standard Czech *párek* refers to sausage bound together in pairs, while *klobása* refers to sausage links. In Texas Czech, *klobasa* refers to both types, and *párek* is largely unheard of. *Prutko* in Texas Czech means "quickly" and seems to have universal applications; it most likely originates from the standard Czech *prudce,* which also means quickly but describes flowing water or wind, never the movements of people. Yet the gentleman whom I heard use *prutko* had never heard of the standard Czech *rychle.*

In addition, there are words and expressions that have become common in Texas Czech that originate from English,[62] either through literal translation or "Czechification":

Texas Czech	English
Šur že jo.	Sure it is.
To je olrajt.	That's all right.
Co viš?	What you know? (Greeting common in rural Texas.)
Daj mi pět.	Give me five. (a handshake, not a hand slap)
severnik	norther (Texas dialect for northern wind)
braunovy	brown, adj.
strobery	strawberry
tomát, tomatíse	tomato, tomatoes
kar	car
korn	corn
sprejovat	to spray, i.e. pesticide
stripovat	to strip (cotton)
pikovat	to pick
kukovat	to cook
kombajn	combine (agricultural machine— The word is also common in the Czech Republic, though it most likely developed independently in Texas)
pinoci	peanuts
hauslik	a little house
stor, štor, stořa	store
melas	molasses
bulik	bull
unca	ounce
puletka	pullet
bodjak	pepper tree, bodark tree —*bodjak* becomes the origin for *bodjač,* which means *thorn*

Though most Czech speakers in Texas will likely understand most of the words above, there is no one form of Texas Czech. Czech speakers around Ennis show a strong Bohemian influence in their speech; many of the words listed above that I heard used around Taylor and Granger originate from Wallachia (V); and some of the Lachian (L) words come from Lavaca County. Hannan has observed strong Lachian influence among Czech speakers in the Granger and Corn Hill areas as well.[63] Also, how the above listed words are used in Texas varies greatly from county to county, even household to household. Yet because of the incorporation of English words and expressions into Texas Czech, and because of the predominant influence of certain aspects of Wallachian and Lachian dialects on the speech of most Czech speakers in Texas, one can argue that Texas Czech has become a distinct dialect with northeast Moravian roots. In his 1976 study, James Mendl came to the same conclusion, stating that "most speakers of Texas-Czech speak not one specific dialect, but a mixture of different dialects. This can be called 'Texas-Czech.'"[64]

At the same time, because of the lack of influence of evolving, standard Czech, and because of the relatively isolated nature of some Texas-Czech communities, many Texas Czechs have preserved the dialect of their parents and grandparents to a significant degree. I remember one gentleman from Frydek, Texas, who astonished native Czechs while he was visiting the Czech Republic because he spoke (so they told me) exactly like someone from Frýdek-Místek. And in the little village of Moravia, Texas, one inhabitant told me he could confirm the traces of three separate dialects, two Moravian and one Bohemian, each spoken by a different local family or group of families. Vestiges of the dialects had survived because each set of speakers spoke

Czech only within the household or among close friends, and, therefore, the different dialects never completely melted together.[65]

Just as Texas Czechs speak their own brand of Czech, so have they to a lesser degree created their own dialect of English. Texas-Czech English is characterized more by its phonological features than lexicographical; it has no single form, shows varying degrees of deviation from standard English, and is most evident in the speech of the older, rural generation. Common features of Texas-Czech English I heard include an absence of correct verb conjugation (e.g., "Was you there too?" and "Oh, he been dead a long time now") and a tendency to finish a question with *not* (e.g., "You was there too, not?").[66] Lexicographical deviations I heard include *somewheres* instead of *somewhere, onliest* in addition to *only,* and the replacement of *still* with *yet* (e.g., "I got to finish the cooking yet"). Some speakers I heard also interchanged *live* with *stay* (e.g., "Oh, you stay in Fayetteville?"), which possibly originates from attempted translation of the Czech *žít* and *bydlet.* Phonological deviations include "t" instead of "th," so that "Thanksgiving" becomes "Tanksgiving," an occasional dental "r," and a tendency to exchange an *-u* sound with *-o,* so that "up" is pronounced "op" and "tunnel" becomes "tonnel." Occasionally I heard stress placed on the penultimate syllable, as in "Gal*ve*ston." The Texas drawl, as well as the East Texas–Southern accent that are perhaps more commonly associated with Texan speech are nonexistent in Texas-Czech English.

The phonological roots of Texas-Czech English lie in its speakers' Czech language. In his study of Sorbian, Polish, and Czech in Texas, Reinhold Olesch concludes that: "the bilingual speaker who belongs to the generation that makes the language change adopts the phonological system of the new language [English] while relating it to the phonological system of his old language [Czech] and ultimately reproducing it with the phonetic realizations of the old language. In this process there operates an illusion of adopting similar phonetic entities even when they have a completely different phonemic function in the old language. This is a decisive factor of linguistic alteration in the phonetic reproduction of the new language."[67]

Probably the most memorable presentation of Texas-Czech English I heard came from some older Texas Germans who were sitting around a little bar in the hamlet of Dreyer in Lavaca County. I asked them what the Czech people were like. "Oh they're good people, hard workin' people," said one, looking at the floor. After a brief silence another remarked: "They talk kind of funny though," and the three old men started to snicker. One imitated a Texas Czech he knew: "I got to go trow de cow owa de fence," he said, and his friends roared with laughter. However, the reader should note that Texas Germans too have their own, unique way of speaking English.

Why has the Czech language in Texas survived to such a remarkable degree? Olesch argues that Slavic languages resist assimilation better than, for instance, Germanic languages, and he also points to the rural nature of the Czech community in Texas.[68] Another reason, perhaps, is that because the Czech language had nearly been eradicated in Bohemia and Moravia under the Austrians, and because the language played such an important part of Czech national identity (as Dongres's quote on page 7 suggests) and the Czech national revival of the nineteenth century, the arriving Czech immigrants felt a stronger responsibility to preserve their language than members of other ethnic groups.

Many Texas Czechs I met were unaware of the significance of their speech, telling me they spoke "slang" or "gutter Czech." Some were even ashamed of the way they spoke, and were reluctant to speak in front of native speakers. Yet one should not underestimate the significance or the unique beauty of Texas Czech. For with its combination of old-country roots and new-world borrowings, Texas Czech is a pure expression of the experience of its speakers—of their history, their identity, and their character.

Fraternals, Sokol, and Press

A variety of Texas-Czech institutions help to maintain a feeling of statewide ethnic solidarity among Texas Czechs, whether through active, organized membership or through subscription to one of the remaining Czech-language newspapers. Each of these institutions has to a varying degree preserved its traditional ties to the Texas-Czech community, though it is the fraternals that wield the most influence. While all (except the Mutual Aid Society) provide different forms of insurance coverage, some also play an active role in promoting the Czech language and Texas-Czech culture and values. The Texas-Czech fraternals and mutual aid societies, in order of largest membership, are:

Rolnický Vzájemný Ochranný Spolek Státu Texas *(RVOS), or Farmers Mutual Protective Association of Texas (founded at Ocker in Bell County in 1901), has 63,586 members and 208 lodges, with its headquarters in Temple.*[69]

Slovanská Podporující Jednota Státu Texas *(SPJST),*[70] *or Slavonic Benevolent Order of the State of Texas (founded at Fayetteville in 1897), has approximately 31,000 members and 130 active lodges, with its headquarters in Temple. The SPJST was the Texas successor to the Česko-slovanský Podporující Spolek (ČSPS), a nationwide fraternal order based in St. Louis, Missouri.*

Česká Římsko-Katolická Podpůrná Jednota Žen Texaských *(KJZT), or Catholic Union of Texas Women —today known as the Catholic Family Fraternal of Texas (founded in 1897 at Yoakum)—has approximately 24,000 members and 128 active lodges, with its headquarters in Austin.*

Česká Římsko-Katolická Jednota Texaská *(KJT), or Czech Catholic Union of Texas (founded at Hostyn in 1889), has 17,125 members and approximately 90 active lodges, with its headquarters in La Grange.*

Slovanský Vzájemně Pojišťující Spolek Proti Ohni a Bouři *(SVPS), or Slavonic Mutual Fire Insurance Association of Texas (founded in Houston in 1926), has approximately seven thousand members and forty-eight Texas chapters, with its headquarters in Rosenberg.*

Podpůrná Jednota Česko-Moravských Bratří, *or Mutual Aid Society of the Unity of the Brethren (founded at Shiner in 1905), is a non-profit organization of approximately twelve hundred members that provides low-interest loans to the twenty-eight Brethren congregations.*

Other Czech-American organizations, such as *Katolický Dělník* (KD, or Catholic Worker), based in New Prague, Minnesota, and the Western Fraternal Life Association, based in Cedar Rapids, Iowa, are also active in Texas.[71]

As mentioned earlier, the fraternals and mutual aid societies were founded by Czechs for Czechs, and have had to adapt themselves to a more and more assimilated Czech community. In fact, the decline of the traditional Czech community in Texas is reflected in the changing policy regarding membership criteria. Directors of the SPJST, for instance, at their second convention in 1899, declared "Only that man or woman can become a member who knows the Slavic (Czech) language. . . ."[72] A 1920 bylaw allowed for the inclusion of non-Czechs, provided one spouse was conversant in Czech, and by 1964, the SPJST dropped Czech as its official language, though in 1980 opening remarks were still in Czech and the convention finished with both "God Bless America" and "Kde domov můj" (the Czech national anthem).[73]

Of the organizations listed above, the SPJST, KJZT, and KJT play the most active role in promoting Texas-Czech culture. Critical to this process are the many fraternal lodges across the state that provide a venue not just for fraternal chapter meetings, but also for tarok tournaments, polka dances, wedding receptions, and family reunions. Some of these lodges, such as the Catholic Czech Club of Dallas—which combines KJT Lodge #111 and KJZT Lodge #108 and has accumulated its own Czech-language library, collection of traditional *kroj*, and pictorial history—have taken their own initiative in promoting their ethnic culture. Investment in its Czech heritage has long been a stated goal of the SPJST; it maintains its own archives and museum of Texas-Czech history in Temple and also provides grants for Czech-language instruction across Texas.

These three fraternals also place great emphasis on their youth programs, which serve not only to promote future membership and fraternal involvement, but also help to maintain Texas-Czech culture and values. The KJZT, for instance, includes Czech singing, crafts, and folk dancing among its junior division activities, and the KJT offers limited Czech-language instruction at its summer camp. The SPJST combines American patriotism, leadership and character building, educational emphasis, and ethnic traditions in its junior division program.[74]

The Texas-Czech fraternals are both agents and a reflection of Texas-Czech culture. By providing membership in an organization whose ethnic roots are both unmistakable and encouraged, they provide important confirmation of an ethnic identity that successive generations of Texas Czechs may begin to doubt. And their dual function as both providers of economic security and social membership strengthens the stability of Texas-Czech communities. At the same time, their spirit of cooperative risk reduction, concern for the well-being of their members, and pride in a shared ethnic identity is characteristic of the values held by the early Czech settlers in Texas. And though the fraternals have adapted in the face of the declining ethnocultural strength of Czech Texas and have expanded their memberships and increased their assets, they have not lost sight of their ethnic origin and responsibility.

One Texas-Czech organization that underwent significant decline but has recently regained viability is the Sokol. Founded in 1862 in Prague to affirm classical ideals of mind and body in combination with Czech cultural and national pride, it spread around the world and first came to Texas in 1907, with chapters at Shiner, Granger, and Hallettsville. It gained quickly in popularity, and at one point had twenty chapters across Texas.[75] Though it lost membership significantly in the post-war years, today there are Texas Sokol chapters at Dallas, Fort Worth, Ennis, West, Taylor, Houston, and Corpus Christi, which attract new members from within and beyond the Texas-Czech community. In contrast to the original Sokol, the Texas Sokols seem to emphasize athletic training more than education, and instruc-tion in Czech history is absent. Similar to the fraternal lodges, some of the larger Sokol halls also serve as venues for social events and ethnic celebrations.

Another institution that has played a critical role in maintaining solidarity among the scattered Texas-Czech settlements and also promoted Czech-language fluency is the Texas-Czech press. Though the fraternals and mutual aid societies continue to publish their own newspapers, only the SPJST's *Věstník* is still published partially in Czech (offering both feature articles and Czech-language instruction). Two other publications, *Našinec* and *Hospodář,* still publish entirely in Czech.

Joe Vrabel, with the help of part-timers Otilie and Marie Maresh, publishes the weekly *Našinec* from the Našinec Publishing Co. in Granger. The paper was originally founded in 1914 in Hallettsville, and later moved to Taylor, where it became the official organ of the KJT. (Today the main publication of the KJT is the English language *KJT News.*) In 1937, it moved to Granger, where it published until closing briefly in 1981, when it was bought by Vrabel, who had been working at the paper as foreman. Working on 1920s-era linotype machines, Vrabel and his two coworkers faithfully print the tabloid paper that is filled with articles written mostly by its readers. Stories, reminiscences, obituaries, recipes, announcements, poems, occasional financial reports by the KJT, and even a little news—as well as advertisements for poppyseed, Czech cookbooks, dictionaries, songbooks, and storybooks—fill *Našinec*'s six pages. Advertisers include the Bluebonnet Nursing Home ("Vaše návštěvy jsou vždy vítáne!" [*sic*]), Rudy Mikeska's BAR-B-Q, Inc. of Taylor ("Máme velice dobré a Čerstvé maso na BARBEQUE . . ."), and Granger National Bank ("Vaše Česká banka"). Vrabel says he stays away from editorials and controversial subjects, which suits *Našinec*'s mostly conservative and elderly readership. Not all writers send their articles in Czech, since not all of them can write the language as well as they can read it. And though Vrabel translates the English articles and corrects the grammar and spelling of the Czech ones, he says he tries not to change passages written in dialect.

Though most issues go to the scattered Czech-settled areas across Texas, some go out of state and even to the Czech Republic. Vrabel also exchanges issues with other Czech-language newspapers in Chicago, New York, and Cleveland. Though readership stood at fifteen hundred when Vrabel took over the paper in 1981, it has since declined to approximately seven hundred and fifty, and Vrabel sees little hope of a radical reversal. With the weekly obituaries of Czech-language speakers in Texas, the paper's eventual demise is certain.

Jan Vaculik is owner, publisher, and editor of Texas' other remaining Czech-language newspaper, the approximately thirty-page monthly *Hospodář* of West. Originally published in Omaha, Nebraska, the paper came to West by fusing with *Čechoslovák* in 1961. Vaculik, a post-1968 émigré from Moravia, came to the paper in 1974 and has been the sole owner since 1989. Like *Našinec*, *Hospodář* is written by its readership, but because its audience is different, the paper as a whole is more intellectual. Stories and reminiscences of everyday life are common in *Hospodář*, as are satire, historical analyses, novellas, poems, travelogues, and articles on public figures. Of the paper's fourteen hundred subscribers, only sixty are in Texas; the rest span across America and around the globe, with about six hundred residing in the Czech and Slovak Republics. Because *Hospodář* has a more diversified base of subscribers, it will likely survive longer than *Našinec,* though its readership too has steadily declined.

Of the two publications, *Našinec* is more typically Texas-Czech, because of its content and style. Though Czech immigrants to Texas had a very high literacy rate compared to other immigrant groups,[76] the vast majority were farmers who had only a basic education, a fact reflected in the paper's present-day readership. However, one should not underestimate *Našinec*'s cultural significance. The paper reflects the character of Texas Czechs, a character that instills *Našinec*'s pages with unpretentious charm and humor despite the often difficult past lives of it writers, lives that were filled with hard work in unforgiving circumstances for uncertain reward.

A crucial aspect of all these institutions, with the exception of the Sokol, is that they were founded in and always identified with Texas. Some, like the SPJST and the KJT, evolved from national Czech-American organizations that did not satisfy the needs of Texas Czechs, while others, like the RVOS, are purely Texas entities. The consequence of this equally Texas and Czech nature is that these institutions solidify a sense of a single *Texas*-Czech identity. Most Texas Czechs I spoke to were aware of Czech settlement in the Midwest, though none seemed to feel significant connection to or solidarity with out-of-state Czech Americans.

Religion

Religion is one of the main cultural features that has differentiated Czechs in Texas from Czechs elsewhere in the United States. Though Texas ranked only sixth in 1910 in its number of first- and second-generation Czechs,[77] during the same approximate period it had more Czech Catholic and Protestant centers than any other state.[78] While both atheistic and agnostic freethought movements that sought to undo traditional ties with organized religion won many adherents in Czech communities from the Midwest states to New York, strongly Catholic and Protestant Brethren parishes flourished in Texas from the beginning of Czech settlement.[79]

Like many aspects of Texas-Czech culture, both the Catholic and the Brethren churches maintained a strong ethnic identity derived from the old-world historical context and new-world social structure. Texas-Czech Catholics especially find strong institutional support for their church among some of the fraternals. Even today the tie between religion and ethnicity, despite efforts by some leaders to lead their church beyond its ethnic roots, remains an intrinsic aspect of many Texas-Czechs' collective identity.

The vast majority of Texas Czechs are Catholic; most Texas-Czech Protestants are Brethren, along with very small numbers of Presbyterians, Methodists, and Baptists. It may seem strange that Catholicism, which after all was the religion of their Hapsburg oppressors, would retain such a large following among Czechs anywhere, though Machann and Mendl point out that the Catholic Church in the Czech lands of the seventeenth and eighteenth centuries managed to associate itself with local national identity.[80] Saints Cyril and Methodius, who brought Christianity to Moravia in the ninth century, have become central to Czech history, and statues of the Czech saints Václav, Ludmila, and Jan of Nepomuk are prominent in Catholic churches throughout Bohemia and Moravia.

As described in Part 1, because so many Czech immigrants arrived in Texas with no knowledge of English, Czech-speaking priests and ministers were in high demand, a need that the Catholic Church in Texas sought to fulfill. Not only did it appeal for Czech priests from Europe, it also established Czech-language programs at seminaries in San Antonio and La Porte. By 1920, with twenty-four Czech priests serving Catholic parishes across the state, there was no demand for English-speaking priests.[81] Many of the Texas churches the Czech Catholics built also reflected their ethnicity, from the paintings and statues of Czech saints to the Czech-language inscriptions on stained glass windows and the stations of the cross.

The KJT and KJZT have provided an important sense of belonging based on religious affiliation that goes beyond the role of the Catholic Church. By taking an active part in the promotion of Texas-Czech culture, the two organizations have created a strong fusion between religious and ethnic identity that also influences successive generations. As the example of Erin Janak (page 82) suggests, youth programs that stress strong personal ties to Catholicism within a context of ethnocultural awareness make the church seem very ethnically oriented to outsiders, a perception that the young participants internalize. And today, even though the Czech-language mass has virtually disappeared in Texas, the singing of Czech songs and the incorporation of parish churches into ethnic celebrations maintain the connection between religion and ethnicity.

Texas' Unity of the Brethren has traditionally adhered to an even stronger connection to its ethnic association than Texas-Czech Catholics. Originally known as the Czech-Moravian Unity of the Brethren, the church was founded in 1457 by Jan Chelčický in Moravia and has its origins among the Hussites, a Protestant group that became very prominent in the Czech lands in the early fifteenth century under the leadership and inspiration of the Czech-religious reformer, Jan Hus.

Chelčický sought to lead his followers toward a simpler, more Christian way of life, one that emphasized education and non-violence. The movement grew in the sixteenth century, and in 1593 finished the first complete Czech-language translation of the Bible, known as the Kralice Bible. Conditions under the Hapsburgs had never been favorable, and the Thirty Years' War proved catastrophic for the Brethren when the Hapsburgs defeated the Czech Protestants at the Battle of White Mountain (Bílá Hora) in 1620. Led by John Amos Comenius (Jan Ámos Komenský), many Brethren followers fled Bohemia and Moravia. By the 1700s the church began to recover after its members found refuge in Saxony. Though the Edict of Toleration of 1781 allowed Czechs to join other Protestant groups, it forbade this privilege to the Brethren, and by the nineteenth century some Czech Brethren were looking to Texas for the salvation of their church.[82]

Czech-Protestant history in Texas begins with the arrival of Rev. Arnošt Bergman in 1850, though it was not until 1864 that Rev. Josef Opočenský established the first Czech-Protestant congregation at Veseli (Wesley). Other early Czech-Protestant communities were founded at Fayetteville, Industry, Shiner, and Vsetin. As the Protestant settlement grew, so grew the desire to unify under a single, organized church, and in 1903, delegates from the scattered Texas congregations met at Granger and voted to establish an independent Unity of the Brethren in Texas. In the ensuing years, members organized the Mutual Aid Society, Sunday schools, and the Hus School, and also brought in other Czech-Protestant congregations. The Brethren also founded its own publication, *Bratrské Listy* (*Brethren Journal*). By 1931, there were thirty-seven congregations in Texas, not including the Brethren congregation at Vsetin that had chosen to remain independent.[83] Nowhere else in America did the Brethren have such a large membership. Though Texas Unity of the Brethren representatives did meet with other North American Czech-Protestant groups, no interdenominational unions were ever established.[84]

Internal dissension over a variety of issues in the 1960s split the Brethren, causing congregations at Placedo, Midfield, Cooks Point, Shiner, and Snook to form their own Brethren denomination. Though some congregations returned to the original Unity of the Brethren, others refused, resulting in separate Brethren congregations, each with its own church, in communities like Buckholts and Temple. Rev. John Baletka, a longtime leader within the Unity of the Brethren, admits the breakup dealt a heavy blow to his denomination. Coupled with declining populations at some of the more rural congregations, the rift has caused a drop in total membership to about twenty-eight hundred in 1993. Baletka anticipates churches at some of the smaller congregations, like Fayetteville and Dime Box, will likely close in the near future, though the Brethren has been successful in efforts to build new congregations, particularly around Houston.[85]

Perhaps because the Brethren was founded in the Czech lands, its Czech heritage seems to have played an even stronger role than in other Texas-Czech institutions. In the *Unity of the Brethren in Texas,* the authors note that "a large number of members were led to equate the Czech language with proper Brethren religious orthodoxy. This view was held by many families for a half century after the 1903 convention."[86] The Hus School, the Brethren summer school meant to guarantee future church leaders, conducted its programs in the Czech language well into the 1940s.[87] One scholar has even described the Unity of the Brethren as an "ethnoreligion."[88]

However, the post-war period seems to represent a shift within the church away from the restrictions of too strong an ethnic identity. In 1959, the denomination changed its name from the Evangelical Unity of the Czech-Moravian Brethren in North America to its present name[89] and later founded new congregations in Pasadena and the Woodlands, areas not linked to traditional Czech settlement. Today the main geographic areas of Brethren membership are the areas around Industry in Fayette County, Seaton and Temple in Bell County, Taylor in Williamson County, Caldwell and Snook in Burleson County, and Wall in Tom Green County.

Though I saw no evidence of tension between Texas-Czech Catholics and Brethren today, several people I interviewed described how intermarriage between the two religious groups was once discouraged from both sides. The Brethren seem to have had a reputation for being more austere than the Catholics; they still drank their beer and danced their polkas, just more demurely. Also, Machann and Mendl suggest a further difference between the two: because most Anglo Americans in Texas have traditionally been Protestant, the Brethren assimilated into Anglo-Texas society more easily than their Catholic compatriots.[90] From an outsider's point of view, this seems true. The Brethren churches I visited, except for the original one at Wesley, which is no longer in use, do not suggest as strong an adherence to an ethnic tradition as many of the Texas-Czech Catholic churches. And except for the history lesson concerning the European origins of the Brethren, the Hus School session I witnessed did not contain a Czech cultural program, a contrast to the KJZT's youth program, which included Czech singing, crafts, and dance. Though the Brethren may have begun in Texas with a stronger ethnoreligious identity, the ethnic component seems to have subsided more quickly with the general Texas-Czech cultural decline of the post-war years.

Texas-Czech membership in other Protestant denominations seems to have come about from early efforts by the Presbyterian Church to organize Czech-Protestant settlers and from the absence of an organized Czech-Protestant congregation in a particular area. In 1915, Rev. J. W. Dobias organized the "Hus" Bohemian Brethren Presbyterian Church in Houston, while the American Presbyterian Church founded congregations at Kovar, Sealy, Rowena, and Brownswood.[91] Of these, the former survived only briefly, while the latter did not actively incorporate ethnicity into its program. Texas-Czech Baptists I met at Macey (northeast of College Station) were among Czech Protestants who joined other denominations because no Czech-Brethren congregation existed nearby.

Relations with Other Ethnic Groups

Despite old-world animosities, Texas Czechs have traditionally had stronger ties to Texas Germans than to any other ethnic group. Language, cultural similarity, and geographic proximity seem to have been the principal contributing factors to this relationship. Because of longtime Austrian rule over Bohemia and Moravia, and because of the many German settlements that existed there since the thirteenth and fourteenth centuries, many more Czechs arriving in Texas knew German than English. Also, some Czech-speaking Germans were among the Bohemian and Moravian immigrants to Texas.[92] Though resentments existed among the first generation settlers (I heard of tension between Germans at High Hill and Czechs at Ammannsville/Dubina, and also between Germans and Czechs around West and Tours), later generations seem to have had little interest in old-world antagonisms. Both cultures in Texas place strong emphasis on hard work and religious devotion, have similar social structure, and have nearly identical tastes in food and music ("…and they're both hard-headed," one Anglo-American observer told me). Though most Texas Germans are Lutheran, a significant number are Catholic, as are most Texas Czechs. In many Texas-Czech settlements, it seems Germans are the largest other ethnic group; every traditionally Czech settlement I visited had Germans within, at most, a ten-mile radius.[93]

As mentioned earlier, the U.S. Civil War pushed the mostly antislavery Czechs and Germans together. It seems many Anglo Americans had trouble distinguishing between the two ethnic groups and did not always welcome the influx of these non-English speaking "foreigners." In 1912, Leroy Hodges observed the success of the "Bohemian" settlers, despite the fact that they were of an ethnic group "of whom so much that is unfavorable is heard at the present time."[94] Hannan also notes: "Some Anglo-Americans seemed to express a degree of resentment that the Czech-Moravian was able to erect such a culturally self-sufficient community on the Texas prairie without great recourse to Anglo-American culture."[95] Because the Czechs were so persistent in maintaining their own culture and language and because they were predominantly Catholic, they came under some harassment from the Ku Klux Klan. In my fieldwork I heard people tell of organized protest by the Klan against the Czechs at West, Granger, Taylor, and Sealy.[96] Many people told me of growing up in mixed Anglo/Czech communities in the 1920s and

1930s and receiving insults from Anglo children at school (e.g., "dumb Bohunk" and "green Bohunk").

The effects of relations between Anglo and other European ethnic groups was significant enough to receive attention by the state government. In 1975, Texas sponsored the Ethnic Heritage Studies Program, a statewide elementary school teacher's guide meant to address the effects of cultural differences. The program abstract states that "for children of Czech, German and Polish descent, who traditionally have felt apart or alien to the dominant culture, it will help develop an individual identity and more positive self-concept based on an open and accepted identification with their heritage."[97]

Today the influence of ethnic relations is still strong. Even younger generation Texas Czechs and Germans seem to mix more easily with one another than with Anglo Texans. Especially in rural areas where the ethnic cultures are still very strong, feelings of ethnic affiliation and difference run deep enough to become quickly apparent, even to an outsider. In my own experience I could usually tell very quickly whether or not someone was Texas Czech, even if he or she did not speak with an accent, for the Czechs were usually more open than the Anglos and more ready to speak with a stranger. I am not from Texas, and the times I felt most out of place or unwelcome were in dealings with Anglo Texans. Some Texas Germans I encountered seemed more suspicious and mistrustful than any Texas Czechs I met, a reaction that did not surprise the Texas Czechs I told of it.

Though pan-Slavism is a quality associated with nineteenth-century Moravian culture,[98] I did not sense that Texas Czechs feel a closer bond to Texas Poles or Wends than with other ethnic groups. Wendish and Czech settlements are in close proximity in Fayette County, and Poles and Czechs have lived side by side in Wilson and Karnes counties (there was heavy Czech settlement around Hobson), and near Brenham and Hempstead in Washington and Waller counties, respectively. The Wends are predominantly Lutheran and have become mostly assimilated into Texas-German culture (and language), while Texas Poles are Catholic and have resisted assimilation more successfully, though not to the same degree as Texas Czechs.[99]

Unfortunately, some Texas Czechs I met had acquired the racist attitude toward African Americans that is still often found throughout America today. Other Texas Czechs I met had a more enlightened attitude toward race, one that judged qualities of individuals rather than groups, and in a manner that did not seem self-conscious.

Overall, it seems that Texas Czechs have less antipathy toward Mexican Texans than toward African Americans, which is perhaps explained by the many cultural similarities between the two ethnic groups. Both are predominantly Catholic; in fact, the abundance of religious icons I saw in many Texas-Czech homes was strikingly similar to traditional Texas–Mexican Catholic domestic culture. Also, both ethnic traditions place strong emphasis on family ties (including *large* families), hard work, and agriculture, and even seem to share a similar love for sausage, beer, and polka music. Also, I was struck by how similar social occasions between the two groups are: a Mexican wedding celebration I observed once in San Antonio, with its polka band, countless family relatives, merrymaking, and overall atmosphere seemed nearly identical in character to a Czech wedding celebration I observed in Weimar.

The strength and charm of Texas-Czech culture has also created its share of ethnic "adoptees." Many non-Czech spouses or even people who have lived among Texas Czechs seemed very drawn by the culture and its powerful sense of identity and belonging. Particularly Anglos, perhaps because they are in the traditional majority and in many ways lack a sense of ethnic solidarity, seem attracted by a culture so rooted in tradition and ethnic identity. If nothing else, certainly Texas-Czech celebrations provide non-Czechs a reason to participate. I remember one man at a polka dance at Seaton who told me, "I've been following these Czechs around for twenty-five years and I've never had so much fun."[100]

Ties to the Old Country

The Velvet Revolution that ended communist rule in Czechoslovakia also created a new chapter in Texas-Czech history. Not only did it enable many Texas Czechs to reestablish personal ties to "the old country," but it also began to restore a sense of cultural and geographic origin that for some had become nearly mythic. Though contact between some families continued after the communist takeover in 1948, by placing the two peoples in enemy camps, the Cold War created a rift much deeper than the physical distance between them. Many Texas Czechs were afraid to visit a communist country; those that did witnessed the stark reality of life under such a system and returned with stories of gray cities filled with sullen faces. For post-war-generation Texas Czechs, the Cold War meant growing up with only a vague notion of a place called Czechoslovakia, a place their ancestors had once known as home but that somehow no longer had its proper place in reality.

The barrier collapsed in 1989, and the nature of the old country changed overnight in the minds of Texas Czechs. Many have since gone over in groups or on their own to finally meet distant relatives, to find the villages of origin of their ancestors or to discover the land they had heard about from their grandparents. Some go to explore specific aspects of their ethnic identity, such as Catholic shrines in Moravia and Poland, or to participate in the recent Sokol celebration. A few have bought property, while younger Texas Czechs have gone to teach English or work in joint business ventures. Older Texas Czechs who still speak the language and have a strong sense of their ethnic and cultural identity seem to fit in very easily, finding a place that is on the one hand very different from their native Texas, yet on the other is culturally very recognizable. Some also return slightly disappointed, for the modern Czech Republic is very different from what their ancestors knew and described. Jan Vaculik of *Hospodář* notes that some Texas Czechs "look for Bohemia and Moravia of a hundred years ago, and are frustrated when the reality doesn't coincide."[101]

Not all Texas Czechs who venture over have a strong awareness of, or even interest in, their ethnic identities. Some I met had gone to pinpoint their genealogical histories but had little desire to affirm their Czech-Moravian selves, while others who had previously resisted the ethnic context of their youth recognized and took pleasure in cultural aspects of their childhood that they had never considered significant before. Also, those who had been largely assimilated in Texas and who yearned to recapture their Czech identity sometimes acquired aspects of Czech culture that were outside the experience of their youth or that of their ancestors. Though their enthusiasm upon their return may help to inject Czech Texas with renewed vitality, what they have learned and seek to share will alter the nature of *Texas*-Czech culture.

Renewed ties have also had a range of effects on Czechs in the Czech Republic. Many native Czechs have already participated in family visitation, student exchanges, informational tours, and technical training in Texas that would have been impossible under the old regime. Dallas and Brno are now sister cities, and La Grange and Frenštát pod Radhoštěm plan to be. Music and dance groups have toured Texas (some also did before the revolution), and the Wallachian Open-Air Museum at Rožnov pod Radhoštěm sponsored its first Texas Day on June 20, 1992, complete with authentic Texas barbecue. The Texas-Czech phenomenon has caught the interest of Czech journalists and scholars, among them Dr. Josef Šimiček, who opened a museum of Czech emigration to Texas in the Moravian village of Lichnov.

Though some Czechs have stayed in touch with their Texas relatives, others are waking up to find Texans on their doorstep claiming to be relatives they never even knew existed. I have heard of encounters that began with suspicion, though once family ties were proven, celebrations that marked the beginning of lasting bonds soon followed. Some villages, particularly in northern Wallachia, have already grown accustomed to the arrival of Texans tracing their roots. In the village of Nový Hrozenkov, the local registrar told me, "It seems in the last three years we have someone from America coming every other day looking for relatives." More and more now I hear of Czech relatives, usually school aged, who have come for six months or a year to stay with Texas relatives, and their presence in some Texas-Czech communities that have never had a "real" Czech visitor for any significant length of time seems disconcerting to some who only know their Texas-Czech experience.

And for Czechs who have never heard of Czech emigration to Texas, encounters with Texas Czechs who look very different but often talk like someone from a nearby village cause confusion and disbelief. I remember one drunken Moravian man who became very angry at a Texas-Czech couple because he was convinced they were 1968 émigrés who had returned now that the political and economic situation in the Czech Republic had improved.

Prospects for the Future

In 1920, Tomáš Čapek wrote, "No parish school, no church organization, no foreign-language community can long withstand the *force majeure* of Americanization. In a measurable time the Bohemias, Germanias, New Braunfels, Polonias and Slovaktowns will be but a name and memory."[102]

Čapek would probably be surprised if he visited Ellinger, Moravia, Granger, or any of the other traditional Texas-Czech settlements today, seventy-four years later, that have so strongly adhered to their culture and language. Why has Czech Texas survived so well when Czech settlements elsewhere in America have yielded to Čapek's *force majeure?*[103] One reason is that of all the states to receive Czech settlers, the Texas population was (and is) the most rural and, hence, the most isolated from the assimilating forces that have swept countless other ethnic cultures into the American melting pot. How else could Toni Barcak of Velehrad or Anna Pelucha of Moravia spend nearly their entire lives in Texas and still, in 1993, have little grasp of (or use for) the English language? Another, just as significant reason, is that nowhere else in America did the Czech community have such a strong institutional base of support: fraternals, mutual aid societies, vernacular press and radio, and now ethnic heritage societies, all of which have retained a firm commitment to the preservation of their culture. Not only have these institutions provided an organized, social context to affirm the individual's sense of ethnocultural belonging, but they also evolved very quickly as specifically *Texas* organizations, and have contributed to the creation of a uniquely *Texas-Czech* cultural identity. Evolution into its own unique form has enabled Texas-Czech culture to survive despite the overwhelming changes within the economic, demographic, social, and cultural context of post–World War II America.

Robert Janak, former president of the Czech Heritage Society, writes: "Czech culture in Texas is not dying. It is being preserved with the greatest of care while undergoing a transformation befitting modern circumstances."[104] The survival of Texas-Czech culture depends on more than the conscious preservation efforts of institutions like his: the culture must also have innate appeal to the next generations. His acknowledgment of "transformation" is apt, for Texas-Czech culture was born from change within transplanted Czech-Moravian culture. As Texas-Czech culture continues to change, it will drift farther away from its original form but will never abandon entirely its ethnic roots. Whether the culture does gain acceptance among the generations of tomorrow remains to be seen, though the level of participation among today's youth is encouraging, as are the renewal of ties to the Czech Republic.

Though hamlets like Velehrad and Bila Hora may fade into oblivion—and the Czech language will likely continue its decline and eventually disappear from active use in Texas—fifty years from now there will still be Texans whose eyes will light up at the opportunity to sing "A já sám" or "Krásná Amerika." A few old men will still address each other fondly with "Co viš, stary ogar?", and a few Texas grandmothers will still prepare kolaches with great devotion. Though Texas-Czech cultural forms may transform or become extinct, it will be much longer before their emotional power has ebbed or their personal significance lost from the experience and memories of Texas Czechs.

Notes

1. Czech speakers will notice some words that seem misspelled. This is because I've typed out the song in accordance with how I heard Mr. and Mrs. Konvicka pronounce the words.

2. Estelle Hudson and Henry Maresh, *Czech Pioneers*, prologue, p. 10.

3. Hudson and Maresh do not cite this report by name. However, they write:

   The United States Department of Labor, Bureau of Immigration, Washington, D.C., in the announcement of permanent residence immigration from Czechoslovakia into Texas during the year ending June 30, 1931, gave the total as 2,016. The preceding year the number was 4,438.

   It is of interest to know that the approximate figure given for total Czech population in Texas in 1932 is between 350,000 and 500,000, prologue, p. 10.

   The numbers 2,016 and 4,438 are to be found in the 1931 annual report, and it is safe to assume that Hudson and Maresh are talking about the next year's issue of the same source, (nowhere else in their book do they cite the source for these figures).

4. See Dongres's account in Machann and Mendl, *Czech Voices*.

5. Terry Jordan, interview by author, Austin, Nov. 1994.

6. This number comes from the Summary Type File 3 (STF3) data base and is arrived at by adding the 136,822 from table P033 (for number of respondents claiming Czech as their first ancestry) and the 54,932 from table P034 (for the number of respondents claiming Czech as their second ancestry). The 90,808 respondents who claim Czech as their only ancestry (table P035) are included in the figure from table P033. According to Mary Kennedy, secretary in the Ethnic and Hispanic Branch of the U.S. Bureau of the Census, people who responded with "Bohemian" or "Moravian" were also coded as Czech.

7. Other states listed in the STF3 data base with Czech populations in excess of 50,000 include (in descending order) Illinois, California, Nebraska, Ohio, New York, Iowa, and Michigan. That Texas should have the highest total is especially interesting in light of figures given in the 1910 census, which ranks Texas sixth (behind Illinois, Nebraska, Ohio, New York, and Wisconsin) in total population of first- and second-generation Czechs. Considering that most emigration to America from Czechoslovakia virtually ceased after 1920, these contrasting figures suggest the vitality of the Texas-Czech community today in comparison to other Czech-American communities.

8. Out of a total Texas population of 16,986,510, the number of people who did not respond, gave an unclassifiable response, or replied only with "American" was 2,681,262.

9. A Czech who changed his or her name to an American one is most likely to have little interest in further association with a Czech or Czech-American identity. See the example on page 19.

10. According to the data in STF3, 13,103,020 people did not respond or could not be classified in table P034.

11. Even in the most rural and traditional areas, marriage between ethnic Czechs and Germans is very common.

12. I arrived at this total by subtracting the number of unreported/unclassified (13,103,020) residents from the Texas total (16,986,510). This identifies 3,883,490 people whose second ancestry was accounted for. Dividing this number into the total of second ancestry Texas Czechs (100,496) gives a percentage of approximately 2.588 percent of Texans whose second ancestry is Czech. Multiplying this percentage times the 13,103,020 who went unclassified gives us 339,106 Texans whose second ancestry is possibly Czech.

13. It is important to note that the number of certificates held by, say the SPJST, does not equal the number of individual members, because a person can have more than one type of insurance policy. Though the SPJST has approximately 51,500 certificates, its actual membership (as of October 31, 1994, according to Vice Pres. Leonard Mikeska) is approximately 31,000. At 63,586 members, the RVOS is the largest of the four. Membership between some of the different fraternals does occasionally overlap, though rarely.

14. Estimates by the fraternals as to the percentage of members who are of Czech descent varied from 65 to 70 percent (in the RVOS) to 85 percent (in the KJZT).

15. A total of 237,557 Texans claim first- or second-Polish ancestry in STF3. However, the number of Poles who emigrated to Texas was lower then the number of Czechs. Also, according to STF3, 48,463 Texans are of

Slovak descent, though only 940 Slovaks are recorded in Texas by 1940 (see Machann and Mendl, *Krasna Amerika*, p. 40).

16. See STF3, 1990 census, table P031, which shows 11,242 Texans who claim to use Polish at home. Both the Slovak and Czech languages are included in the category of "other Slavic," though of the 21,952 respondents, 20,453 claimed Czech (see the following section on language).

17. Hannan, "Study of the Culture."

18. Generally, Bohemians and Moravians of the nineteenth century accepted that they were both of the same national group. Hannan notes, however, that this idea had much less currency in northeastern Moravia, where so many of the immigrants to Texas were from. For a discussion of differences in meaning between the terms "Moravan" and "Moravec," see Hannan, "Study of the Culture," 11.

19. See the Dongres account in Machann and Mendl, *Czech Voices*, pp. 116–17.

20. This is as mentioned by Hannan "Study of the Culture," pp. 12–13 and Dongres (in Machann and Mendl, *Czech Voices*, p. 117).

21. I remember one exception in particular. While driving through the settlement of New Taiton in Wharton County, I stopped at little Kahanek's Cafe to ask whether many Czechs still lived in the area. The woman behind the counter looked at me suspiciously and said no and that Czechs had never lived in that area. Puzzled, I asked if she was Czech. "No," she replied, "I'm Moravian." "Are there many Moravians in this area?" I asked. "A few," she answered.

22. Mary Kennedy, interview by author, telephone conversation, Nov. 1994.

23. Hannan "Study of the Culture," 2.

24. Many pre–World War I and even pre–World War II English language accounts of Czechs in America, whether written by Czechs or non–Czechs, favor the term "Bohemian."

25. While there are several places called Písek in Bohemia and Moravia, I'm sure he was referring to somewhere in Texas rather than Europe.

26. For a further discussion of reaffirmed ethnic identity, see the example of the Dallas and West dance groups in the following section on Texas-Czech culture.

27. James Darilek, interview by author, Gonzales, Texas, Apr. 4, 1993.

28. CHS descriptive flyer, 1993.

29. For more information on early folklore, see Olga Pazdral's indispensable "Czech Folklore in Texas" (master's thesis, the University of Texas at Austin, 1942).

30. For original Czech recipes, see Joza Brizová and Maryna Klimentová, *Czech Cuisine.*

31. For a more complete account of Baca history, see Cleo R. Baca, *Baca's Musical History: 1860–1968,* or go by Baca's Historic Saloon and Confectionery in Fayetteville. According to Cleo Baca's text, Antonín Dvořák, descendant of the famous Czech composer, played briefly in Joe Baca's band in 1912.

32. See the photo of Ray Krenek on page 57. The Moravian dulcimer is very different from the smaller instrument with the same name common in Appalachian-Anglo folk music.

33. One of the original Krenek dulcimers used by Ray Baca has been preserved at the Fayetteville Museum in Fayetteville, Texas.

34. Leland Miller, interview by author, Fayetteville, Texas, Nov. 12, 1993. I first heard the term used by Miller, general manager for Kovanda's Czech Band of Houston.

35. The Leo Majek Band will celebrate its one-hundredth anniversary in 1997.

36. Leland Miller, interview.

37. Lee Roy Matocha, interview by author, Fayetteville, Texas, Nov. 16, 1993.

38. For a partial listing of Czech-Moravian and Texas-Czech folk songs see the Dallas Czech Singers, *Pisnicky České: Czech Folk Song Collection.*

39. See the Konvicka family, page 20.

40. Clinton Machann, "Czech Folk Music, Orchestras, and Assimilation in Texas," *Kosmas* issue no. 7, (1988): 107.

41. Ibid., 110.

42. Maggie Grmela, interview by author, West, Texas, May, 1994.

43. See the photograph on page 53.

44. See the photograph on page 25. For a brief discussion of the *kroj,* see Willa Mae Cervenka's "Parade of Authentic 'Kroje' Costumes from Czechoslovakia" in KJT, *Centennial Celebration.*

45. One example stands out in particular of a young man from the Dallas area. On the back of his ornate vest was embroidered the name "Květoslav," which he told me was his Czech nickname, though he would not elaborate on why he chose to be called that. Transla-

tion: "One who celebrates flowers." It was once a fairly common name in the Czech lands.

46. See the foreword in Barbara Dybala's *Generation to Generation: Czech Food, Customs, and Traditions, Texas Style.*

47. John Kebrle, interview by author, Dallas, Texas.

48. Toni Knapek, interview by author, Granger, Texas. See also the photo on page 43.

49. STF3 of the 1990 Census of Population and Households, table P031 under Texas, shows more speakers of German, French, French Creole, Vietnamese, Korean, Chinese, Tagalog, and Indic than Czech.

50. STF3 lists Polish, Russian, South Slavic, and Other Slavic among languages other than English spoken at home. "Other Slavic" was chosen by 21,952 respondents. According to Rosalind Bruno, statistician in the Education and Social Stratification Branch of the U.S. Bureau of the Census, of these, 20,453 responded with Czech (responses such as "Bohemian," "Moravian," and "Maehrisch" were also coded as "Czech").

51. See Anna Pelucha on page 75. Toni Barcak, born in Texas, of Velehrad in Lavaca County, is another example.

52. See Smith's conclusion in his "Demise of Czech."

53. Bill Vornsand of Schulenburg, page 24, is a perfect example.

54. Ben Jurica, interview by author, Velehrad, Texas, Apr. 10, 1993.

55. Among these were Arthur Dobbins of La Grange, who died around 1986, and Thomas Burns of Abbott, who died around 1983. Ludvík Dongres, a Czech-American journalist writing in 1924, claimed that children of several African-American families living around Fayetteville spoke "Moravian" better than English (see Machann and Mendl, *Czech Voices*, p. 128).

56. Kevin Hannan, "The Moravian Speech of Texas," *KJT News* (March, April, May, 1992). Hannan points out that only *Svoboda* published some of its readers' letters in the original dialect in which they were submitted.

57. See Dongres's account in Machann and Mendl, *Czech Voices*, p. 117, as well as the captions for Joe and Annie Martinek, page 81.

58. Hannan, "Moravian Speech."

59. Hannan, personal correspondence, Nov., 1994. Hannan identifies these forms as *přehláska*, a vowel shift in the Czech language that occurred in the Middle Ages and has determined contemporary vowel pronunciation in standard Czech.

60. For additional words found in Texas Czech, see Kevin Hannan's "Dictionary of Texas Moravian," Department of Slavic Languages, University of Texas at Austin, unpublished.

61. Jiří Langer, personal correspondence, from series of interviews and letters, June–October, 1994. Dr. Langer, who supplied the origins of these words, is the ethnographer at the Wallachian Open-Air Museum, Rožnov pod Radhoštěm.

62. For additional Texas-Czech words of English origin, see Margaret Cunningham Kutac, "English Loan Words in Texas-Czech" (master's thesis, the University of Texas at Austin, 1967).

63. Hannan, "Moravian Speech."

64. James Mendl, "Texas Czech: Historical Czech Dialects in the New World" (master's thesis, the University of Texas at Austin, 1976), 51.

65. Thadious Polasek, interview by author, Moravia, Texas, Oct. 1994.

66. Probably the purest, most beautiful Texas-Czech English I heard spoken came from Lawrence Korenek, Sr. (see page 26).

67. Reinhold Olesch, "The West Slavic Languages in Texas with Special Regard to Sorbian in Serbin, Lee County," in *Texas Studies in Bilingualism: Spanish, French, German, Czech, Polish, Sorbian, and Norwegian in the Southwest*, 151.

68. Olesch, "West Slavic Languages."

69. Membership totals for all the fraternals are as of October 1994.

70. One man I spoke to laughingly referred to the SPJST as "Special People Jesus Selected for Texas."

71. For the histories of the KJT, KJZT, and KD in Texas, as well as other Texas-Czech Catholic fraternal organizations that no longer exist, see Národní Svaz Českých Katolíku v Texas, *Naše Dějiny*.

72. Nick Morris, *A History of the SPJST: A Texas Chronicle, 1897–1980*, p. 27.

73. Ibid.

74. The KJT and KJZT also encourage future leadership within the Catholic Church by offering scholarships for seminarians, while the SPJST is a strictly secular organization that disallows discussion of religious issues at its meetings.

75. The Sokol was seen by some as anti–Catholic, result-

ing in the creation of the Orel (*sokol* means "falcon" and *orel* means "eagle"). Orel chapters in Texas existed briefly at West, Ennis, and Penelope. In addition to the three chapters mentioned, there were Sokols at Ennis, Waco, Dallas, Fort Worth, Penelope, Guy, Seaton, Buckholts, Houston, Crosby, Rowena, Galveston, Corpus Christi, Placedo, Floresville, San Antonio, and East Bernard.

76. Bruce Garver, "Czech-American Freethinkers on the Great Plains, 1871–1914," p. 147; and Machann and Mendl, *Krasna Amerika.*

77. As mentioned previously, the 1910 census gives a total of 41,080 first- and second-generation Czechs in Texas. Illinois, Nebraska, Ohio, New York, and Wisconsin all claimed more.

78. Vera Laska, in *The Czechs in America, 1633–1977: A Chronology and Fact Book,* cites Tomáš Čapek's *The Czechs (Bohemians) in America: A Study of Their National, Cultural, Political, Social, Economic, and Religious Life.* Texas had 68 of the nation's 320 Czech Catholic and 43 of the 160 Czech-Protestant centers. See also Čapek's example (p. 119) of religious affiliation among Czechs in New York, of whom 62 percent claimed no religious affiliation at all.

79. Machann and Mendl, *Krasna Amerika,* chap. 4; and Garver, "Czech-American Freethinkers on the Great Plains, 1871–1914." Though the SPJST is a freethought organization, it is not anti–Catholic or anti–Brethren, and is not driven by an anticlerical ideology.

80. Machann and Mendl, *Krasna Amerika,* chap. 4.

81. Ibid., p. 111.

82. Christian Sisters Union Study Committee, *Unity of the Brethren in Texas (1855–1966).*

83. Ibid., p. 66.

84. Though they cooperate in their missionary efforts, the Unity of the Brethren in Texas and the Moravian Church, based in Bethlehem, Pennsylvania, are two completely independent entities.

85. John and Joyce Baletka, interview by author, Caldwell, Texas, June 4, 1993. See also the supplement to the Christian Sisters' *Unity of the Brethren.*

86. Christian Sisters, *Unity of the Brethren,* p. 163.

87. John and Joyce Baletka, interview.

88. Richard Machalek, "The Ambivalence of Ethnoreligion," in *The Czechs in Texas: A Symposium, Temple, TX, October 27–29, 1978,* Ed. Clinton Machann.

89. Christian Sisters, *Unity of the Brethren,* p. 32.

90. Machann and Mendl, *Krasna Amerika,* p. 116.

91. Hudson and Maresh, *Czech Pioneers,* p. 217, and Machann and Mendl, *Krasna Amerika,* p. 124.

92. I already mentioned that there were Czech-speaking Germans around Velehrad in Fayette and Lavaca counties. Among these was the Schwartz family that emigrated from Moravia, specifically from the area east of Olomouc where there were German settlements at Potstadt, Odry, Ziebenthal, Siegerstau, and Schmiedsau. I met Czech-speaking Texas Germans in Lavaca County, Ammannsville, and Ellinger.

93. For further accounts of relations between Texas Germans and Czechs, see Mollie Emma Stasney, "The Czechs in Texas" (master's thesis, the University of Texas at Austin, 1938), and Machann and Mendl, *Krasna Amerika.*

94. Leroy Hodges, "The Bohemian Farmers of Texas," *Texas Magazine* 6, no. 2 (June 1912): 91.

95. Hannan, "Study of the Culture," p. 34.

96. Mildred Naizer, seventy-four, of Granger, told me when the Klan came through Taylor "We'd go hide 'cause we were scared" (interview by author, July 8, 1993). However, I never heard of any violence committed by the Klan against Czechs.

97. Southwest Educational Development Laboratory: Ethnic Heritage Studies Program, *Czechs in Texas.*

98. Hannan, "Study of the Culture."

99. For more information on Texas Wends, see Anne Blasig, *The Wends of Texas;* George Nielsen, *In Search of a Home: The Wends (Sorbs) on the Australian and Texas Frontier;* George C. Engerrand, *The So-Called Wends of Germany and Their Colonies in Texas and in Australia;* as well as the Wendish museum in Serbin, Texas. For more information on Texas Poles, see Miecislaus Haiman, *The Poles in the Early History of Texas* and Joseph Jaworski, *Panna Maria: An Image of Polish Texans.*

100. Lee Roy Bates, interview by author, Seaton, Texas, July 25, 1993.

101. Jan Vaculik, interview by author, West, Texas, Feb. 20, 1993.

102. Čapek, *Czechs (Bohemians),* p. 113.

103. One very notable though isolated example is the Czech community of Spillville, Iowa.

104. Robert Janak, "Czech Texas and the Texas Czechs," *Stirpes* 31, no. 3 (Sept. 1991): 119.

Part 4

Into the Old Country

Alden Smith, Dan Pustejovsky, and Margie Collins were among a group of Texas-Czech Catholics to visit the annual Saints Cyril and Methodius celebration at Velehrad in the Czech Republic. Many native Czechs are unaware of the heavy Czech presence in Texas and often received the above group with curious looks, warm greetings, and occasional tears. These Texans were among an increasing number of Texas Czechs who are traveling to the Czech Republic to search for relatives, to find the villages where their ancestors came from, or to simply see the country. Group leader Smith said he felt so at home that he bought a house in southern Moravia to escape the hot Texas summers.

Since the 1989 political revolution in the formerly communist Czechoslovakia, Texas Czechs are journeying to the Czech Republic in greater numbers than ever before, the vast majority in search of relatives. Some, like Marjorie Matula of Victoria (opposite page, above), who found her husband's relatives in the Moravian village of Hajov, are successful, while others find clues to help them when they come again. "It's okay, we'll just come back next year," said one searching Texan, Lydia Ondrias. Whether they meet with success or temporary failure in their searches, most Texas Czechs leave eager to return. "You go for a couple weeks and make friends for life," said Lydia.

Leo and Rita Janak of Shiner got a warm reception from Leo's relatives (above) who live in the little village of Tichá in northeastern Moravia. The Janaks's visit in 1994 marked the fourth time they have traveled to the Czech Republic. When they first came in 1979, they were guided only by a house number on an old letter, which brought them to the door of Hanka Maralík. Rita remembers that Hanka and her husband, Ferdinand, were suspicious of her and Leo and didn't believe they could be relatives. Though when an old photograph of Maralík relatives matched one the Janaks had brought, the Maralíks's suspicion disappeared. "At that moment a door opened, it was such a feeling," says Rita. Since then the Maralíks have been to Texas twice for Janak family reunions. "We were so surprised at all the nice Czech songs they know, even more than us," says Hanka. Opposite page, below, Rita bids farewell to Ferdinand and Hanka after a few days' visit.

Not all Texas Czechs come to the Czech Republic for a quick tour. El Campo native Jane Reynolds (above), inspired by the changes that overwhelmed Eastern Europe in 1989, taught high school English in the coal and steel producing town of Karviná for one year. "There was just something exciting about coming over here in a country that's just starting out," she says. Living in the Czech Republic has required its adjustments but also presented familiarities to Reynolds. "A friend of mine in Texas asked me 'What do Czech people look like?' and I said, 'Well, Barbara, they look like people in El Campo.'"

Some Texas Czechs arrive in the Czech Republic eager to explore other aspects of their ethnic identity. Rome Milan (above), of the Sokol chapter in Fort Worth, came with a Texas delegation to the annual *Slet*, or celebration, that unites Sokolites from around the world. The Sokol had been banned by the Czechoslovak communists, and the 1994 *Slet* in Prague marked a new beginning for the organization. "It was absolutely fantastic," says John Kebrle, a Sokol representative from Dallas. "They haven't had a *Slet* in Prague in over forty years, and here we were to be a part of it."

The Czech Heritage Society of Texas sponsored its own summer tour, which included three weeks of classes in Moravian folk arts and Czech language at the Wallachian Open-Air Museum in Rožnov pod Radhoštěm. Opposite page, above (left to right), David and Steve Labay of San Antonio and Tria Molberg of El Campo learn to paint eggs using wax, and above Henrietta Cervenka of Waco confronts Saints Cyril and Methodius at a nearby museum. "We want people to share what they've learned once they come back to Texas," said CHS president Caroline Meiners.

At the Wallachian Open-Air Museum in Rožnov, officials built a Texas pioneer log cabin (opposite page, below) for their permanent exhibit in time for the first Texas Day in 1992, which drew several hundred Texans and boasted authentic barbecue.

As contact between Texas and the Czech Republic is strengthened, the phenomenon of Czech-Moravian emigration to Texas is catching the interest of Czech scholars. Dr. Josef Šimiček, from the little village of Lichnov in northeastern Moravia, became so interested in emigration from his area that he opened a small museum that includes lists of names of emigrants and their villages of origin. Above, he assists Texan Marjorie Matula to locate possible relatives. Another Czech, Drahomír Strnadel, mayor of the little Moravian village of Trojanovice, first became interested in emigration to Texas when a friend told him about the one hundred families who had gone there from Trojanovice. Strnadel began to compile a list of emigrants, and in 1989, he and a film crew went to Texas for two months to do a documentary film for a local television station. "We felt at home there," he says. "I could live there and die there."

Many Texas Czechs who journey to Moravia are fluent in Czech and communicate easily with natives. Among the more gregarious in the Czech Heritage Society group was Alphonse Budnik of Bay City, who amused locals with jokes and Texas antics. Many Czechs are greatly surprised not only by how well some Texans speak Czech, but also by the regional, Moravian dialects evident in the way they speak.

Andrea Babincová, eighteen, of Frenštát pod Radhoštěm, first met distant cousin Anna Krpec (above, third from left) and other Texas relatives in 1991. "We didn't know anything about them. They were so strange to us at first," she said. "But then last summer, Anna said I could come to live with them for a year if I wanted. At first I thought it was unreal. I mean, it's not every day that someone asks you to come to America."

Her parents (above) admit they were hesitant. "We were a little scared," said her father, Karel. After living with her relatives and going to school for a year in Houston, Andrea has no doubts about the strengths of her new ties. "I love them," she says of her Texas relatives. "Even if they weren't really family, they'd be family to me."

Appendix

Settlements in Texas with Czech-Derived Names[1]

Settlement	County	Still Exist?[2]	Settlement	County	Still Exist?[2]
Anton	Hockley	Yes	Hegar	?	?
Barta (Bárta)	Colorado	No	Holik (Holík)	Waller	No
Besa	Lavaca	No	Holub	Victoria	No
Bila Hora (Bílá Hora)	Lavaca	Yes	Horak	Austin	Yes
Bohemia	Tom Green	No	(Horák, now Cat Spring)		
Bohemia Colony	Jim Wells	No	Hostyn by Ellinger	Fayette	Yes
Settlement			(Hostýn, now St. Mary's Church)		
(also Kostohryz)			Hostyn (Hostýn)	Fayette	Yes
Bordovice	Fayette	No	Hovezi	Fayette	Yes
Branecky	Fayette/Gonzalez	No	(Hovězí, now Plum)		
Brno*	Liberty	No	Hranice	Lee	Yes
Budejovice	Fayette	No	Hruskaville	Bell	No
(Budějovice)			(Hruškaville)		
Cechtice (Čechtice)*	Wood	No	Jelebenka	Lavaca	No
Chupikova Zahrada	Atascosa	No	(also Yellow Bank)		
(Chupiková Zahrada)*			Kasprlink	Austin	Yes
Dubina	Fayette	Yes	(Kasprlink, now Cat Spring)		
Frenstat (Frenštát)	Burleson	Yes	Kaznicov (Kazničov)*	Fayette	No
Frydek (Frýdek)	Austin	Yes		or Lavaca	
Frydlant (Frýdlant)	DeWitt	No	Klimek	Fayette	No
Haiduk	?	?	Kocicina (Kočičina)	Fayette	No
Hajek (Hájek)	Baylor	No	Komensky	Lavaca	Yes
Halenkov*	Brazos	No	(Komenský)		

Settlement	County	Still Exist?[2]
Kopecky (Kopecký)*	Fayette	No
Kopecky Town (now Elmaton)	Matagorda	Yes
Kopecky Town (probably Rye)	Brazos	No
Kosarek (Kosárek)	?	?
Kovar (Kovář)	Bastrop	Yes
Krajina	Lavaca	No
Krasna (Krásná)	Fort Bend	Yes
Kubala	DeWitt	No
Lipa (Lípa)	?	?
Liskův Haj (Lískuv Háj)*	McMullen or Live Oak	No
Lysa Hora (Lysá Hora)*	McLennan	No
Machovec[3]	Moore	No
Marak (Marák)	Milam	Yes
Marekville (now Six Mile)	Calhoun	Yes
Matula	Lavaca	No
Moravan (now Hostyn)	Fayette	Yes
Moravia	Lavaca	Yes
Mikeska	Live Oak	Yes
Nechanitz	Fayette	Yes
Neusserville	Williamson	No
New Tabor (New Tábor)	Burleson	Yes
Nova Morava (Nová Morava)*	Brazos	No
Nova Osada (Nová Osada, now New Colony)	Milam	Yes
Novohrad	Lavaca	Yes
Nykel (now Nickel)	Gonzales	Yes
Olomouc*	Brazos	No
Orech (Ořech)*	Fayette or Colorado	No
Petras*	Ellis	No
Pisek (Písek)	Colorado	No
Polanka	Williamson	No
Pokrok Flats*[4]	Tom Green	No
Prague	?	?
Praha	Fayette	Yes
Praha*	McLennan	No
Psencik (Pšenčík)	Fayette	No
Radhost (Radhošť)	Lavaca	No
Radhost (Radhošť)	Fayette	No
Ratibor (Ratiboř)	Bell	Yes
Rek Hill (Řek Hill)	Fayette	Yes
Rosanky	Bastrop	Yes
Roznov (Rožnov)	Fayette	Yes
Sebesta (Šebesta, now Snook)	Burleson	Yes
Shimek (Šimek)	Lavaca	No
Sliva (Slíva)*	Fayette or Colorado	No
Smetana	Brazos	Yes
Srnec*	McMullen or La Salle	No
Sulak (Sulák)	Lavaca	No
Svata Anna pri Yoakum (Svatá Anna při Yoakum, now St. Anne's)	DeWitt	Yes
Tabor (Tábor)	Brazos	Yes
Tyn (Týn)*	Jackson	No
Ujetov (also Hewitt's Place)	Washington	No
Velehrad	Fayette/Lavaca	Yes
Veseli (Veselí, now Wesley)	Washington	Yes
Vlastenec	Lavaca	No
Vlkov (now Ammannsville)	Fayette	Yes
Vsetin (Vsetín)	Lavaca	Yes
Vysehrad (Vyšehrad)	Lavaca	Yes
Wokaty (also Vokaty)	Milam	No
Zabcikville (Žabčíkville)	Bell	Yes
Zizkov (Žižkov)	Bell	No

Notes to Czech Name Settlements

1. Names with an asterisk (*) are from names of RVOS lodges. Glenn Hutka, president of the RVOS, said these were most likely named after nearby communities, though further information was unavailable. Other sources for these settlement names include Hessoun, *Kratké Dějiny a Seznam Česko-Katolických Osad ve Spoj. Státech Amerických;* Morris, *History of the SPJST;* Christian Sisters, *Unity of the Brethren;* KJT, *Centennial Celebration;* Hudson and Maresh, *Czech Pioneers;* Jelinek, *Lavaca Co.; Fayette County Courthouse and Communities;* and Texas A&M University Cartographics Library, *The Roads of Texas.*

2. The term "exist" needs clarification. Some of these places have little physical vestige to prove they are there beyond a cemetery or a few farmsteads. Yet they possess a sense of place for locals, who may still refer to them as geographic entities.

3. I include this only because it is a Czech sounding name. According to Mrs. Bert Clifton, director of the Moore County Museum, Machovec is a railroad switch named after a yard foreman on the Fort Worth and Denver Railroad during the 1930s and 1940s.

4. Glenn Hutka of the RVOS suggested that this might have been a name for the flatland east of San Angelo around Wall.

Bibliography

Allen, J. P. and Turner, E. J. *We the People: An Atlas of America's Ethnic Diversity*. New York: MacMillan Publishing Co., 1988.

Anderson, Benedict. *Imagined Communities: Reflections on the Origin and Spread of Nationalism*. London: Verso Publications, 1983.

Arbingast, Stanley et al. *Atlas of Texas*. Austin: University of Texas Bureau of Business Research, 1976.

Baca, Cleo R. *Baca's Musical History: 1860–1968*. La Grange, Tex: La Grange Journal, 1968.

Barthes, Roland. *Camera Lucide*. New York: Hill and Wang, 1981.

Bartoš, Evelyn, and Aneška Bartoš. *Spivejme Pisni čky*. N.p.: Privately printed, 1976.

Becker, Howard S. "Photography and Sociology." In *Doing Things Together: Selected Papers of Howard S. Becker*. Evanston, Ill.: Northwestern University Press, 1986.

Belicek, Rozie. "The Story of My Life." Unpublished manuscript, 1972.

Bell County Historical Commission. *The Story of Bell County, Texas*. Vols. 1 and 2. Austin: Eakin Press, 1988.

Benjamin, Gilbert G. 1910. Reprint, *The Germans in Texas: A Study of Immigration*. Austin: Jenkins, 1974.

Berger, John, and Jean Mohr. *Another Way of Telling*. New York: Random House, 1982.

Biesele, R. L. "The History of the German Settlements in Texas, 1831–1861." Ph.D. diss., University of Texas at Austin, 1930.

Blasig, Anne. *The Wends of Texas*. 1954. Reprint, Brownsville, Tex.: Springman-King Printing, Inc., 1981.

Boethel, Paul. *History of Lavaca County*. Austin: Von-Boechmann Jones, 1959.

Břizová, Joza, and Maryna Klimentová. *Czech Cuisine*. Prague: Avicenum, 1985.

Bujnoch, Dorothy, and Anne Rhodes. *Czech Footprints Across Lavaca Co.: 1860–1900*. Vol. 1. N.p.: Privately printed, n.d.

Čapek, Tomáš. *The Czechs (Bohemians) in America: A Study of Their National, Cultural, Political, Social, Economic, and Religious Life*. New York: AMS Press, 1920.

Cervenka, R. W. *John Kohut and His Son Josef, Czechoslovak Countrymen in Early Texas*. Waco, Tex.: n.p. 1966.

Chervenka, Calvin. "Reference Information Concerning the Czechs of Texas." Dallas: Privately printed, 1977.

Christian Sisters Union Studies Committee. *Unity of the Brethren in Texas (1855–1966)*. Taylor, Tex.: Unity of the Brethren, 1970.

Collier, John, and Malcolm Collier. *Visual Anthropology: Photography As a Research Method*. 1986. Reprint, Albuquerque: University of New Mexico Press, 1990.

Conzen, Kathleen Neils. "Historical Approaches to the Study of Rural Ethnic Communities." In *Ethnicity on the Great Plains*. Edited by F. C. Luebke. Lincoln, Neb.: University of Nebraska Press, 1980.

———. *Making Their Own America: Assimilation Theory*

and the German Peasant Pioneer. New York: Berg Publishers, 1990.

Czech Catholic Union of Texas. *The Czech Catholic Union of Texas, 1889–1989: Centennial Mass of Thanksgiving and Dedication of Monument, Holy Rosary Church, Hostyn, Texas, July 2, 1989.* N.p., 1989.

———. *Short History of the K.J.T.: 1889-1973.* N.p., 1973.

Dallas Czech Singers. *Pisničky České: Czech Folk Song Collection.* Kingwood, Tex.: Kay Graphics, 1985.

Dongres, L. W. "Paměti starých českých osadníků v Americe." In *Amerikán Národni Kalendař.* Chicago: Nakl. Ing. Geringera, 1924.

Dybala, Barbara. *Generation to Generation: Czech Food, Customs, and Traditions, Texas Style.* West, Tex.: Čechoslovák Publishing Co., 1980.

Engerrand, George Charles. *The So-Called Wends of Germany and Their Colonies in Texas and in Australia.* Austin: University of Texas, 1934.

Fayette County Courthouse and Communities. Schulenberg, Tex.: N.p., n.d.

Fayetteville Bank. *A Short History of Fayetteville, Texas and the Surrounding Communities.* N.p., 1976.

Flach, Vera. *A Yankee in German-America.* San Antonio: Naylor Company, 1973.

Freeman and Doty Associates. *Wesley Brethren Church: Historic Structures Report.* Technical report, 1980.

Garver, Bruce. "Czech-American Freethinkers on the Great Plains, 1871–1914." In *Ethnicity on the Great Plains.* Edited by F. C. Luebke. Lincoln: University of Nebraska Press, 1980.

Gloeckner, Annie Mae. *The Czechs in Wharton County.* Pierce, Tex.: Privately printed, 1985.

Goethe-Institut. *Lone Star & Eagle: German Immigration to Texas.* Houston: Goethe-Institut, 1983.

Goodwyn, L., W. Watriss, and F. Baldwin. *Coming to Terms: The German Hill Country of Texas.* College Station: Texas A&M University Press, 1991.

Gorzycki, Bruno, ed. *History of St. Mary's Parish.* Brenham, Tex.: n.p., 1986.

Haiman, Miecislaus. *The Poles in the Early History of Texas.* Chicago: Polish R. C. Union of America, 1936.

Handler, R., and J. Linnekin. "Tradition, Genuine or Spurious." *Journal of American Folklore* 97, no. 385 (1984): 273–90.

Hannan, Kevin. "A Study of the Culture of the Czech Moravian Community of Texas." Unpublished manuscript, 1985.

———. "The Moravian Speech of Texas." *KJT News.* March, April, May, 1992.

Harper, Douglas. "Visual Sociology: Expanding One's Vision." *American Sociologist* 19 (Spring 1988): 54–70.

Hejl, Edmond. *Czech Footprints across the Bluebonnet Fields of Texas: Villages of Origin—Protestant.* Fort Worth: Privately printed, 1983.

———. *Czechs and Moravians in Texas.* N.p., 1983.

Hessoun, Josef. *Kratké Dějiny a Seznam Česko-Katolických Osad ve Spoj. Státech Amerických.* St. Louis, Mo.: n.p., 1890.

Hewitt, William P. *The Czechs in Texas: A Study of the Immigration and Development of Czech Ethnicity, 1850–1920.* Ph. D. diss., University of Texas at Austin, 1978.

———, ed. *The Czech Texans.* San Antonio: University of Texas Institute of Texan Cultures at San Antonio, 1972.

Hodges, Leroy. "The Bohemian Farmers of Texas." *Texas Magazine* 6, no. 2 (June 1912): 87.

Hrncir, Charles, and Marilyn Hrncir. *Joseph and Anna Svoboda Hrncir Family.* Austin: Privately printed, 1991.

Hudson, Estelle, and Henry Maresh. *Czech Pioneers of the Southwest.* Dallas, Tex.: Southwest Press, 1934.

Hunaček, Václav. *Czechoslovakia: Information Minimum.* Austin: Texas Education Agency, 1970.

Janacek, John. *Saints Cyril and Methodius, Dubina, TX, Diamond Jubilee: 1877–1952.* 2d ed. Dubina, Tex.: Privately printed, 1979.

Janacek, John E. *Czechs and Others at East Gate, Liberty Co., TX.* Yorktown, Tex.: Privately printed, n.d.

Janak, Robert. "Czech Texas and the Texas Czechs." *Stirpes* 31, no. 3 (Sept. 1991).

———. *Dubina, Hostyn, and Ammannsville: The Geographic Origin of Three Czech Communities in Fayette County, Texas.* Beaumont, Tex.: Privately printed, 1978.

———. *Geographic Origins of Czech Texas.* Beaumont, Tex.: Privately printed, 1985.

———. "Proudly Czech and Irrevocably Texan." *Ročenka* 1, no. 1 (Winter 1992).

———. *Simiček, Šugarek, Janák.* Beaumont, Tex.: Privately printed, 1976.

Jaworski, Joseph. *Panna Maria: An Image of Polish Texans.* Wimberley, Tex.: Dorsoduro Press, 1991.

Jelinek, L. W. *Map of Lavaca Co.* N.p., 1896.

Jerabek, Esther. *Czechs and Slovaks in North America—A Bibliography.* New York: Czechoslovak Society of Arts and Sciences, 1976.

Jochec, Jesse. "The Life and Career of Augustin Haidusek."

Master's thesis, University of Texas at Austin, 1940.

Jordan, Terry. *German Seed in Texas Soil: Immigrant Farmers in Nineteenth Century Texas.* Austin: University of Texas Press, 1966.

———. *Population Origin Groups in Rural Texas.* Washington, D.C.: Association of American Geographers, 1970.

Kennedy, Carol, Linda F. Butler, and Marianne McCann. "Churches in Texas with Decorative Interior Painting." Austin: Texas Historical Commission, 1983.

Laska, Vera, ed. *The Czechs in America, 1633–1977: A Chronology and Fact Book.* Dobbs Ferry, N.Y.: Oceana Publications, 1978.

Lotto, F. *Fayette County: Her History and Her People.* Schulenburg, Tex.: Sticker Steam Press, 1902.

Lum, Casey Man Kong. "Communication and Cultural Insularity: The Chinese Immigrant Experience." *Critical Studies in Mass Communication* 8, no. 1 (March 1991): 91–101.

Machann, Clinton. "Czech Folk Music, Orchestras, and Assimilation in Texas." *Kosmas* issue no. 7 (1988): 107–12.

———. "Texas Czechs Preserve a Proud History." *Texas Humanist* 1, no. 4 (Dec. 1978): 1.

———, ed. *The Czechs in Texas: A Symposium, Temple, TX, October 27–29, 1978.* College Station: Department of English, Texas A&M University, 1979.

Machann, Clinton, and James Mendl, eds. *Czech Voices.* College Station: Texas A&M University Press, 1991.

———. *Krasna Amerika: A Study of the Texas Czechs, 1851–1939.* Austin: Eakin Press, 1983.

MacKenna, L. W., and A. Berend. *Saint Thomas Parish, 1891–1941: Pilot Point, TX.* Pilot Point, Tex.: n.p., 1941.

Malik, Joe. "Efforts to Promote the Study of the Czech Language and Culture in Texas." Master's thesis, University of Texas at Austin, 1947.

Marek, Thomas W. Untitled essay, 1992. Barker Center for American History, University of Texas at Austin.

Maresh, Henry R. "The Czechs in Texas." *The Southwestern Historical Quarterly* 50 (1946): 238.

Matula, Nancy. "Nemeceks: A Czech Meat Market." *Texas Historian* 34, no. 4: 12.

McCandless, Barbara. *Equal Before the Lens: Jno. Trlica's Photographs of Granger, Texas.* College Station: Texas A&M University Press, 1992.

Mendl, James. "Texas Czech: Historical Czech Dialects in the New World." Master's thesis, University of Texas at Austin, 1976.

Mikulencak, Maudy. "Hej Slovane!" *Texas Highways* 35, no. 8 (Aug. 1988): 36.

Morkovsky, Alois J. *Short Biographies of Czech and Other Priests in Texas.* Hallettsville, Tex.: Privately printed, 1982.

Morris, Nick. *A History of the SPJST: A Texas Chronicle, 1897–1980.* Temple, Tex.: Slavonic Benevolent Order of the State of Texas, 1984.

Národní Svaz Českých Katolíků v Texas. *Naše Dějiny.* Granger, Tex.: Našinec Publishing Co., 1939.

Nielsen, George R. *In Search of a Home: The Wends (Sorbs) on the Australian and Texas Frontier.* Birmingham: Department of Russian Language & Literature, University of Birmingham, 1977.

Ogg, Jimmie Rene. "Holik." In *Former Post Offices of Waller Co.* Edited by M. W. Abshier et al. N.p.: Waller County Historical Society, 1977.

Olesch, Reinhold. "The West Slavic Languages in Texas with Special Regard to Sorbian in Serbin, Lee County." In *Texas Studies in Bilingualism: Spanish, French, German, Czech, Polish, Sorbian, and Norwegian in the Southwest.* Edited by Glenn Gilbert. Berlin: Walter de Gruyter and Co., 1970.

Pazdral, Olga. "Czech Folklore in Texas." Master's thesis, University of Texas at Austin, 1942.

Perkowski, Jan. "A Survey of the West Slavic Immigrant Languages in Texas." In *Texas Studies in Bilingualism: Spanish, French, German, Czech, Polish, Sorbian, and Norwegian in the Southwest.* Edited by Glenn Gilbert. Berlin: Walter de Gruyter and Co., 1970.

Prochaska, Alvin. "Czechs in Nueces County." *Nueces County Historical Commission Bulletin* 2, no. 1 (Nov. 1989): 39.

Roemer, Ferdinand. *Texas; With Particular Reference to German Immigration and the Physical Appearance of the Country.* San Antonio: Standard Printing Company, 1935.

Saint John the Baptist Parish. *History of St. John the Baptist Parish, 1890–1990.* Schulenburg, Tex.: n.p., 1990.

St. Mary's Parish, High Hill: 125th Anniversary. Schulenburg, Tex.: n.p., 1985.

Schulenburg Sticker. *The High Hill Centennial History.* Schulenburg, Tex.: n.p., 1960.

———. *St. Mary's Parish: 1840–1990.* Schulenburg, Tex.: St. Mary's Church, 1990.

Shils, Edward. "Tradition." *Comparative Studies in Society and History* 13 (1971): 122–59.

Šiller, V., V. Průcha, and R. de Costello. *Památník Českých Evanjelických Cirkvi v Sev. Americe.* Chicago: n.p., 1900.

Silverthorne, Elizabeth. *Christmas in Texas.* College Station: Texas A&M University Press, 1990.

Skrabanek, Robert L. "Czechs in Texas in 1980." *Věstník* (March 21, 1984): 10.

———. *We're Czechs.* College Station: Texas A&M University Press, 1988.

Smith, Connie Sherwood. "The Demise of Czech in Two Texas Communities." Ph.D. diss., University of Texas at Austin, 1991.

Southwest Educational Development Laboratory: Ethnic Heritage Studies Program. *Czechs in Texas.* Austin: The Laboratory, 1975.

Špaček Family. *Památník Rodiny Špačkové a Jejich Spříbuzněných Rodin.* N.p.: Privately printed, 1931.

Splawn, Vlasta. "Sociological Study of a Czech Community in Ellis County, Texas." Master's thesis, Texas Tech University, 1972.

Stasney, Mollie Emma. "The Czechs in Texas." Master's thesis, University of Texas at Austin, 1938.

Strnadel, Drahomír et. al. *Tam za mořem je Amerika.* Vratimov, (Czech Republic): Polykart, 1992.

Students of La Grange High School. "Fayette County: Past and Present." Whitehead and Whitehead, 1977.

Svrcek, V. A. *A History of the Czech-Moravian Catholic Communities of Texas.* Waco, Tex.: Texian Press, 1974.

Texas A&M University Cartographics Laboratory. *The Roads of Texas.* Fredericksburg, Tex.: Shearer Publishing, 1988.

University of Texas Institute of Texan Cultures at San Antonio. *The German Texans.* 1970. Reprint, San Antonio: University of Texas Institute of Texan Cultures at San Antonio, 1987.

———. *The Polish Texans.* San Antonio: University of Texas Institute of Texan Cultures at San Antonio, 1972.

U.S. Bureau of the Census. *Census of Population and Housing, 1990.* Bureau of the Census. Washington, D.C., 1993.

———. *Fourteenth Census of the United States: 1920.* Bureau of the Census. Washington, D.C., 1923.

———. *Population of the State of Texas: Final Figures.* Bureau of the Census. Washington, D.C., 1943.

———. *Sixteenth Census of the United States: 1940. Nativity and Parentage of the White Population: Mother Tongue.* Bureau of the Census. Washington, D.C., 1943.

Valchar, Jerry E. *History of the Farmer's Mutual Protective Association of Texas, RVOS.* Temple, Tex.: n.p., 1982.

Webb, Walter Prescott, ed. *Handbook of Texas.* Austin: Texas State Historical Association, 1952.

Weyand, Leonie Rummel, and Houston Wade. *An Early History of Fayette County.* Austin: Eakin Press, 1936.

Winfield, Judy and Nathaniel. *Cemetery Records of Washington County: 1826–1960.* N.p.: Privately printed, 1974.

Wright, Jody Feldtman. *Czechs in Grey and Blue, Too!* San Antonio, Tex.: J. F. Wright, 1988.

Wyman, Mark. *Immigrants in the Valley: Irish, Germans and Americans in the Upper Mississippi Country, 1830–1860.* Chicago: Nelson Hall, 1984.

Zelade, Robert. "Room to Grow." *Texas Highways* (Sept. 1993): 56.

Index